Crusader Publications
980 Timothy Ave.
Carlisle, Ohio 45005

 For information address: Crusader Publications 3481 S. Dixie Hwy Suite 309 Franklin, Ohio 45005

For information about special discounts for bulk purchases, please contact Crusader Publications or email FromDarkToNarc@gmail.com

Crusader Publications can bring this Author to your live event. Contact us
At: From Dark To Narc @gmail.com or:
At our website: www.fromdarktonarc.com

Website Designed by Michael Stahr at running2win.com.
Edited by Ms Courtney Goffinet and Mrs. Barbara Goffinet
Book Cover Design by Terri J. Brewer at Fadedxstar@gmail.com
Manufactured in the United States of America

0 9 8 7 6 5 4 3 2 1
ISBN 978-0-9910074-0-0

To Milton Union Library
Gary Goffinet

CONTENTS

JOHN EDGAR HOOVER MEMORIAL AWARD
DISTINGUISHED POLICE SERVICE
06/02/2007

PROLOGUE

The name of the book is (From Dark to Narc), and I made the decision to name the book this way because it is the beginning of good times, bad times, the darker times, lighter times, and the learning times of my life. I wanted to tell the story of how I was able to get through all of those times so I could continue my life with dignity.

I hope through these writings that I may help someone else to achieve a better life and be able to accomplish changing his or her life for a better tomorrow, and that they may start using their head for something other than a hat rack. A person can accomplish more than he can imagine by using the legal systems that this country and states have adopted.

I really wanted to get this book written and published, if at all possible, before my father passed away. I loved my father more than anything in life and respected his teachings so much. It was with great sorrow that I was unable to do so because he passed June 9, 2005.

He was always behind me and taught me so much about construction and how to work on cars. I wanted more than anything for him to see that I made it in life, as a good and decent man.

I want to share my story with those people who have made mistakes as they've traveled through life and they just can't seem to let go in their thoughts and actions.

As you follow my travels, you will find that it is never too late to make things happen to improve your life and make you the person you want to become.

THIS IS ME AT OR ABOUT 4 MONTHS OLD

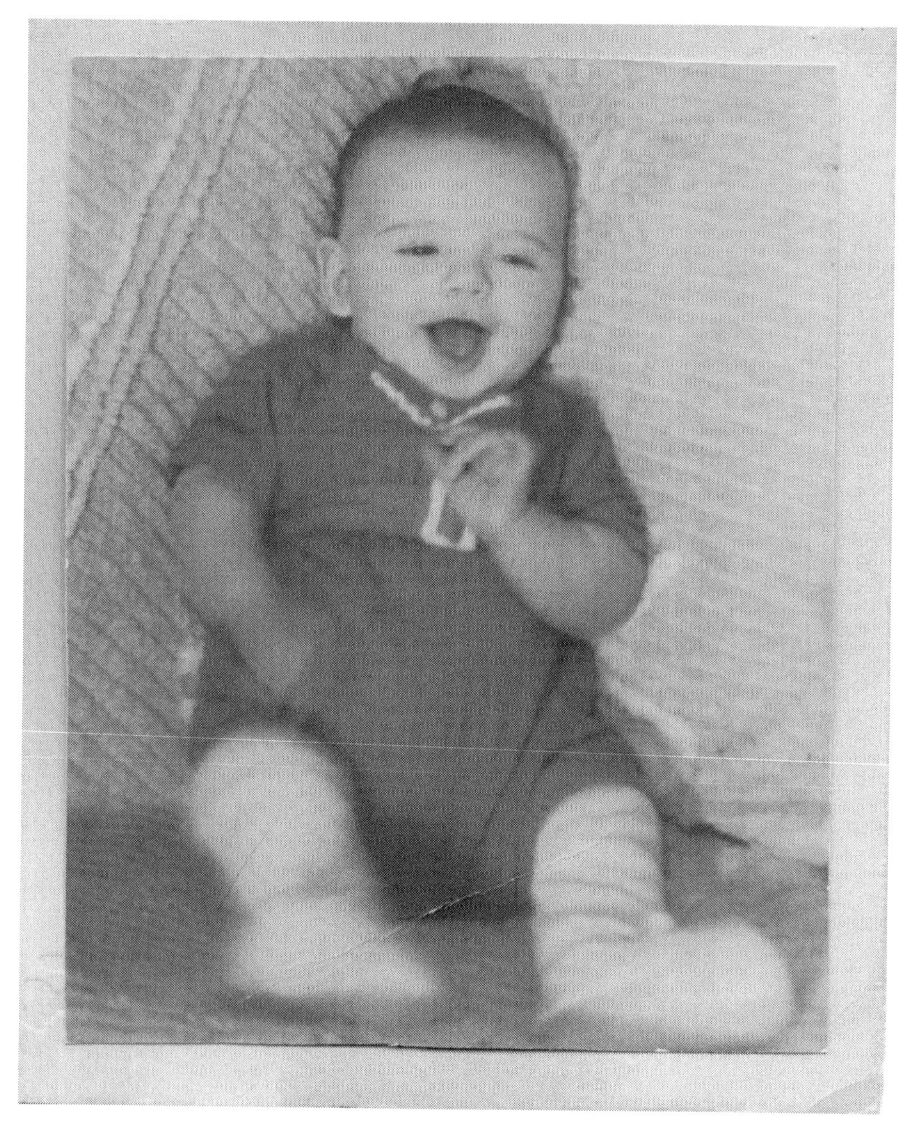

STARTING LIFE

The first house we lived in as I remember it, was a three room cabin where I had to sleep in the same room with my older brother and sister. My mom and dad slept on a hide-a-bed that was our living room couch during the day and mom and dad's bed during the night. Let me say, that if these arrangements were to happen in this time of life, my parents would have been jailed for child endangerment or something stupid. You would have been considered a pervert or even worse. This is the time in life when some friends and I were running and generally screwing around the house when I tripped and fell into a big pile of glass in the back yard and cut myself pretty good on my right arm. Later in life I told a big lie about being shot in a bar while working undercover in Montgomery County, Ohio.

This is when I found out just how easy it was to mislead people into believing just about anything if you had the right props.

Later on in my life I told the story that I was accidentally shot in some bar brawl and I just showed them the scars and said the bullet entered here and exited there. This line of crap and others sure helped later in life when I felt my life depended on making believable stories to really make sense.

I still remember as far back as when I was about nine years old, my younger sister and I fought just about all the time. We fought over marbles, bicycles, balls, candy, and everything we touched. I guess that was just a normal brother-sister relationship. Over the years, I have seen other children doing the same thing.

She and I have never been that close and damned if I can figure out why. If she needed anything or my help to this very day I would be there for her, she just never has asked.

A story comes to mind when I was about 6 years old. I was looking for something to do and decided to build a make believe ranch house out of some large cardboard boxes. These boxes came from some new furniture my folks had bought for our home.

At the time, we lived in Irvington, Ohio on top of a small hill. Our home was the middle of three homes in a row. We had a small stand of woods behind our homes.

I sat the boxes up so that they faced forward into a spot that I had cleared of leaves and brush. I made sure the flaps opened and shut like doors. When I finished building it, I decided it needed a fence around it, so I went to my dad's garage and found a roll of blue string in one of his tool boxes. I then weaved the string between trees and bushes all the way around my make-believe ranch house.

I had left the area of my make believe ranch home to go to the bathroom. While I was gone, my sister tore down the whole damn thing. Why? Who the hell knows! I always knew she was just downright mean and sneaky.

This was my first lesson in life of "trusting" people. I still never have in 71 years, figured out how to read people's minds, especially my sisters.

Our houses that sat on the hill overlooked a garden that belonged to the parents of a friend of mine whose name was Curtis.

There was a large garden between my house and his house. His parents had cultivated what I would call today, a truck patch. They spent a lot of time out there growing corn and tomatoes and I'm sure other stuff as well.

I remember David, another friend of mine, and I were hiding in that garden and throwing rotten tomatoes on the back porch of Curtis's house. We laughed like the dickens when we watched them splatter all over their back porch and on the side of their house.

Heck, it was Halloween and we were just doing pranks at the time. Curtis's dad came out of the house and had a really pissed off look on his face.

He started yelling that he was fed up with our pranks and threatened to turn his dogs loose to find out who was in the garden. David and I jumped up and started yelling, "don't turn the dogs loose, we give up!"

We ended up having to clean all the rotten tomatoes off of his back porch and off of the side of his house. I don't know what David's dad said to him, but my dad took my bike away from me and restricted me to my house and property. He did not let me associate with David for two weeks.

All of our neighbors were really great people and treated us kids great. When Halloween season arrived, we never pushed over their outhouses or soaped their windows. I cannot say that I never got involved in pushing over a few outhouses in my younger days; I just didn't help push over anyone's that were friends of my father's or treated me nice as I grew up.

One outhouse that comes to mind is: when it fell over, it just collapsed into a big pile of junk wood! The old guy that owned it was calling the cops and just raising all sorts of hell. He was causing such a ruckus that one of the guys that helped push it over got scared and told his dad.

That's when all of us kids had to fork up the money to buy material to rebuild this guy's crapper. When it fell over, the roof just laid over on the ground as if it was a puppy rolling over to get its belly rubbed. The walls folded over like dominos as it completely collapsed flat on the ground!

My allowance, for the rest of the year, was used to help pay for my part of the materials, or it seemed that way at the time, because I could not go to the movies with my mother, brother, and sister for two or three weeks.

One of the most memorable times of pushing over outhouses happened to an elderly gentleman and his wife who lived just a couple of blocks from my house in Laura, Ohio. His actual name was Barney, who was most likely seventy five years old, had silver hair and always had stubble for a beard.

I still remember him sitting at the Sinclair gas station where the soda fountain was and bragging that nobody was going to push over his outhouse. He had it wired down to big steel stakes that had been driven in the ground at each corner. I was thinking maybe we should "check this out" and found, he indeed, was telling the truth!

It seems he forgot that there was a tool called "bolt cutters" in some of our dads' tool boxes. It pushed over so easy that afterwards we were afraid the old guy may have been in it and did not have a chance to yell or anything!

We did not hear any yells or screams all evening so we assumed he was not in the outhouse with Sears Roebuck catalogs piled up around him! I can still hear him today, sitting at the soda fountain, yelling and cussing about those little bastards pushing over his crapper!

He was never heard bragging about keeping his crapper upright again, so no one wanted to push over his outhouse any longer. From that day on, when trick-or-treaters showed up at his house we always got some great treats and a nice smile.

I was always able to make these silly stories into some fantastic tails and was able to make things sound so much more interesting in my life. I told a tall tale about blowing up this crapper with a stick of dynamite that I had stolen from a stone quarry just outside of our little town.

I had stolen that stick of dynamite and a blasting cap from the stone quarry that was just outside of town a couple of miles. I told how I had cut it in half and placed it under the crapper with the blasting cap inside of it. I told how I had run my dad's extension cords down the alley to a barn where we played all the time and used a tractor battery to detonate the explosive. I told how it left a big hole where the crapper was and how it sent a smelly substance all over the block!

This story simply wasn't true at all and was just a figment of my great imagination.

I did many things that could have injured or killed me or my friends that no person knows about to this day. The ones that my mother and father did find out about resulted in fair and justifiable paddling or some other kind of punishment. Thank God they did not find out about all the things my brother and I did. I would most likely still be grounded to the house to this day!

The new laws about a parent who disciplines his children in an old-fashioned way by using his belt across the rear end of his child, is the ruination of all morals in our lives today, I'm sure! I'm against a father or mother who uses a ball bat or big stick to punish or abuse a child to the point of making bruises on the child. I'm so against tying the kid to a bed or locking him or her in a closet.

These are methods of punishment that should never be tolerated in any civilized nation. It turns my stomach when I hear of a criminal, in front of the courts, lay blame for his "breaking of the law" on his folks because of the way he was raised. They go out and get high on drugs or alcohol, get stupid and rob ten or fifteen dollars off of some poor person who was just walking his dog while enjoying a sunny day at the park.

I could never blame my parents for any of my stupidity. They were very hard working people who took very good care of all of us.

We had our vacations every year, and went to the Great Smoky Mountains more than once. The trip was always great and the view was absolutely beautiful when you looked out over the clouds and could see the misty fog in the early morning hours.

I remember going to the Cherokee Indian Reservation in North Carolina. A short time after arriving there, a bridge had collapsed, killing a couple of people.

The last time I was there the bridge was still closed to the public and I don't know as of yet if it has ever reopened.

We were still able to see the Indians and shop all the souvenir shops and get our pictures taken with the Indian chief in front of his teepee at the reservation.

We also traveled to Leopold, Indiana at least once a year, to see my uncles and aunts on my dad's side of the family. Uncle Victor was my favorite because he had a great pond. He allowed us to swim in it all the time.

He also had this little service station with one of the first soda cooling machines I can ever remember. You would put a nickel in and you had to slide the bottle over to a notch and lift it out. If you somehow stopped and let the bottle drop back down, you would lose your nickel **and** the bottle of soda. My uncle always gave us the soda anyway. It was still the neatest machine I had ever seen at this time in my life. I was always getting nickels from my mom to play with it.

Now when we went to visit with my dad's relatives, all the people would get together and start playing cards and drinking a few beers. My dad did drink on rare occasions. I remember him and my Uncle Victor drinking one night and my dad got what I thought was pretty drunk. He decided to walk to Tell City, Ind. which was a long way from where Uncle Victor's home was. Later that night, after we realized that he was gone too long, my brother and I decided to go look for him and headed toward town to find him.

We found him just lying in the ditch beside the road. We helped him into the car and took him back to Uncle Victor's house where he was safe again. He did catch a lot of grief from my mom though!

My Uncle Lester also lived in this area of Indiana. His farmhouse had a red clay driveway and the red dust would fly when the cars would drive on it.

I will never forget those meals that were made back then. There was always a big table with more gravy and biscuits than ten people could possibly eat. The bacon was so much bigger and better pieces than you can buy now. The eggs were fried in good old lard and they were so good I could eat a half dozen and not bat an eye.

I guess I'm going to die from all the calories, saturated fats, and bad stuff that were in all that food. It's funny though that all of my grandparents, great-grandparents, aunts and cousins all seem to be living a good life without food related illnesses.

Vacations were always fun. Even way back then we heard the old sayings, "are we there yet?" And, "I got to go pee." Times have not changed that much with some things. My children did the same thing when they were growing up.

My mother was a very kind and gentle woman who really knew how to get things done and how to make sure us kids toed the line.

The times that we spent together are forever implanted in my mind. I remember the time we went fishing and picnicking along the creek that ran alongside St. Rt. 55 just outside of Ludlow Falls, Ohio. It was a very warm day in mid August; we were picnicking and having roasted marshmallows over a fire.

My mom had made a fire out of some dried up sticks that we had gathered up from the woods.

While roasting my marshmallow over the fire, the stick my marshmallow was on was over top of my sister's marshmallow stick.

Somehow, hers caught fire about the same time as mine did and when she jerked hers out of the fire, her stick struck mine and my marshmallow mysteriously stuck to my forehead, still flaming! Damn that hurt! I still have a scar to this day!

My mother always fished with a small string and a hook and it seemed she was always able to catch three or four fish along the bank. This was always a lot of fun and I always looked forward to our picnicking days.

My father worked in Dayton, Ohio at a steel forging plant where they forged crankshafts for automobiles, trucks, airplane engines, airplane propellers, and I guess a lot of other things. I do remember going there a couple of times when dads' factory had "bring your child" day to share your job with them. Seeing these large forging hammers that were steam powered, hammering large blocks of red hot steel into rounded forms and later turned into crankshafts, was a sight to see.

Dads company picnics were absolutely the greatest and we had a lot of fun every year that we went.

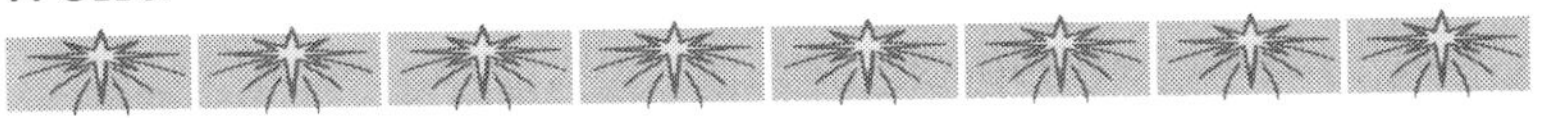

We had three-legged races and played all kinds of games where we won prizes such as bikes, skates, games and other great gifts. My brother and I won new bikes one year after winning a three legged race tied together at the ankles. All the adults and other children were yelling and screaming, having as much fun as I.

We had hot dogs and hamburgers, chips, cakes, pies and just about everything else you could think. Homemade food always tasted so good!

My father enjoyed life to its fullest. He spent so much time in the garage with my brother and me just fixing bikes, scooters and old cars. It was the grandest of times as we always seemed to have a lot of fun just being with him. Dad was always teaching my brother Bill and I what the different parts of an engine was and how they worked to make it run correctly. Later on in life I ended up losing a car down in Kentucky. You would think I would have known better than to let a car run out of antifreeze! He taught me better than that! Dad had this little car called a Crossly, which I believe was made by Sears and Roebuck, I'm not really sure. It was a little tiny car. I believe it was smaller than a Volkswagen.

The story goes that one night while dad was at work some of his coworkers picked the car up and put it between two light poles so he could not get it out when he got off work. He told me what they had done when he got home that night.

He told mom about it later on that night while they were bowling. The bowling league was a big part of my dad's life. He was an avid bowler and bowled nearly every Friday night with a group of his coworkers.

Dad retired from the foundry and promptly got a job at a gas station called Barns Sohio in West Milton, Ohio. Being the jokester that he was, he proceeded to hook up a "spark plug testing tool" to a metal strip which was attached to a workbench. I think he created the first actual taser!

If he saw you leaning against the workbench, he always seemed to find a reason to be around the "spark plug testing machine". The next thing you knew, you were getting the shock of their life!

He even got the local cop a few times and to this day I don't think Harman Miller, the Chief of Police at the time, ever figured it out. Chief Miller was a heavy set man who was at most about five feet six. I always thought he should play Santa. Those days were the greatest and I hope that I will never forget them. I hope to always be able to close my eyes and in the darkness try to relive them over and over again.

I don't think my father ever got mad at anybody. He always seemed to be in a great mood and enjoyed life and what it had to offer.

He loved to fish, bowl, and mess around with old cars and to this day I never work on a car that I don't remember something that my dad showed or taught me. He did all of this and still had time to take us fishing. He tried to get us to be quiet so we would not scare the fish. He taught me to watch the little red and white bobber that always told you when a fish was trying to get the worm off the hook. He taught me how to "sink" the hook into the fish as the bobber went down.

As I grew older, I got my first two wheel bike. It was an eighteen or twenty inch bike with solid rubber tires. My Uncle Ted was the first to try and ride it, what a joke! Uncle Ted must have weighed 250 lbs, and I still can't figure out how it stayed together! The way I remember it, the tires even got flatter when he got on it, if that was even possible!

STARTING SCHOOL

I started my schooling at Northmont Elementary in Englewood, Ohio. Our school colors were green and white. My first grade teacher's name was Mrs. Furnas, a very nice lady with silver hair. She probably got that silver hair by many previous children she had encountered before me.

At that time, all teachers seemed to be at least 90 years old, to me. When I go to the school with my granddaughter now, I see teachers that can't be more than twenty two or twenty three years old. They are very nice young men and women.

First grade was so long ago. I remember chocolate milk was only two cents! I remember all the great times we had at recess! Because it had been so long ago, I can't remember all the names of the kids I went to school with, but I do remember Curtis, Larry, and David. They just lived a few houses down from where we lived. I ran and played with these guys till my family moved to Ludlow Falls, Ohio sometime in 1952.

I started attending Milton Union School in West Milton, Ohio in the fourth grade. It wasn't long before I had my first run in with a teacher.

Her name was Mrs. Rose and to this day I can't recall what started this problem, but rest assured it was most likely my fault.

I was probably running my mouth as most ten year olds do. She gave me a couple whacks with the paddle and as I returned to my seat, another student told her that I had stuck my tongue out at her. That just did not happen! Nevertheless, she decided I did and proceeded to paddle me some more!

I then took the paddle away from her and started paddling her as she ran from me around the room. The same person who lied on me, tried to trip her by sticking his foot out as she passed him going around the room.

I really caught the dickens and a real paddling from the principle when she finally got the paddle from me. I believe this was one of the "lighter" bad things that I did in my early school years.

I remember playing "kick the can" in the middle of the intersection under the streetlight at night. Every day I wonder why children are more interested in hi-tech games than fellowshipping, laughing and having a good time with their friends. What happened to "kick the can"?

It seems all you hear is "I'm bored, there isn't anything to do." It just seems that when I was growing up, we always found something to do, even if it was being a little ornery.

Getting high on drugs never entered our minds. We got high on having fun and doing things like pushing over outhouses, putting trash in the local police officers patrol car while he was inside having coffee at the local ice cream stand, and other mischievous things.

Well, as I sit here thinking of all the silly stuff I've done over the years to get myself into and out of trouble, I find myself wanting to jump forward a few years and just skip the different stupid things I did in my adolescent life. Stupid things, like hanging out of cars upside down or jumping off the bridge into Ludlow falls and other really crazy fun things.

The fact remains that a loving mom and dad, who did not mistreat me or abused me in any way known to man, brought me up to be a decent human being. At the time, I just didn't seem to catch on. I was more interested in just being a butt.

The things that have happened in my life were created through no one's fault but my own. The fact is, in time, these events made me a much better man.

Through a lot of hard work, loss of family and jobs, my life has still worked out to the good and I thank God for that each and every day. Oh yes, I do believe in the Almighty and his son Jesus Christ.

Maybe someday, sometime, or somewhere, a person who takes the time to read these words, will find a new path in life to follow and will know that whatever happens in one's life does not always remain the same. You truly can overcome bad things.

I recall a guy that my older brother ran around with when I was in grade school. Although my brother was a few years older than I was, we still hung pretty close and I knew most all of his friends as he did mine.

This friend of my brother's, his name was Bill Dallas. He lived three blocks from us. The reason Bill Dallas hung with me was because he was always doing stupid stuff just like me! After school he would ride on the back of the school bus to our house! He would climb on the back of the bus, stand on the bumper, and hang onto the lights. He looked like Jesus on the cross as he rode down the road toward our house. This was when school buses had bumpers on them and big taillights that stuck out the back. To this day I can't figure how the driver did not see him hanging on the back of that bus!

Bill and I would get together and build carts. We made them from two by fours and old buggy wheels (yes, it really did happen). We spent hours riding down a big hill that was just a short distance from our house. Those were some of the greatest of times.

My parents would see to it that all of us kids got what we needed in life. Maybe not everything we wanted, because even then, people lived from week to week on their paychecks just to feed, clothe, and keep the bills paid.

We all looked forward to school. Two or three weeks before school started, mom and dad would take us to Rikes in downtown Dayton, Ohio. They would buy us all new school clothes and shoes. We used to get home and try on everything we got just to see how good we looked. It was so much fun; we just couldn't wait till school started so we could wear them.

The school always seemed to be so clean and smelled so fresh; like it had just been painted.

I remember seeing all the new teachers and all my friends on that first day.

Sometimes we met new friends but we also hung out with our old friends. We began the school year with tons of anxiety on new things to increase our knowledge.

Well, most of the kids did. I guess I was a little different than most. I liked sports and gym class. I only carried about a “c” average in school. I remembered getting into a few fights with the other kids in class, but nothing ever serious. We would get a black eye once in a while and maybe a bloody nose. There was a whole lot of yelling and name calling.

The best looking teacher we had in school was Mrs. Dunn. She taught typing class and all the guys wanted to go to typing classes for that reason. They only lasted a short time in her class because they would ask her questions just to get her to lean over their shoulder! Oh well!! Boys will be boys!

My latter school years were not bad either. I can still recall going on class trips. One of the trips was to the Miami Valley Milk Producers Association and another one was to the Pepsi Cola plant.

We always got free milk, bread, or pop and items for souvenirs. It seemed we always got a plastic magnifying glass everywhere we went. The guys tried their best to start fires with them. If you let the sun shine through it onto a piece of paper, it would burn the paper. I've heard stories about guys trying to fry grasshoppers, but I could never get one to hold still long enough to get it fried! Schools have just about stopped taking the children on field trips now days. Insurance and liabilities are the main reason, let alone those pedophiles that are lurking out there.

Fun times in high school also included mooning people or hanging -ten as it's called today. Every time I listen to Jeff Foxworthy tell his funny stories, it brings back memories of the fun we had. Anyone can surmise that I had more fun-time than learning-time in school!

Hindu tag was a game we played in high school and the only safe position was on your toes, fingertips and your nose. You always knew who got out of line in Health class. Mr. Gin, who taught Health class, also taught gym class. Gym class followed Health class and Mr. Gin was the first person to be "it". Mr. Gin went after the guy who screwed up in health class, first. Mr. Gin stood over him till his belly hit the floor. The poor guy got a whack to his posterior with a paddle!

The poor guy became "it" and the game continued from there. When gym class was over, everyone headed to the showers. You were able to see who got whacked because they had a case of the "red butt."

Some of the friends I hung out with in school were, Dale, Vernon, Stanley, Rantz and a few others. Boy, did we have great times.

I think we did everything from playing war to jumping out of barns with umbrellas. Some of these escapades would amount to a book in itself! One escapade I remember very vividly.

It was close to Halloween. Stan, Vernon, Dale, and I were at Stan's house. We found a cat wondering around in the back yard and decided to have some fun. We caught the cat, jumped in Stan's car and took off down the road at fifty or sixty miles per hour. Vernon tossed the cat out. We all wanted to see if the cat had landed on its feet. So, we turned around and found out that indeed, a cat does have nine lives. The cat landed on its feet and seemed to be in great shape. Last thing I remember was that the cat was going into a cornfield and wasting no time getting the hell out of there.

When I read in the paper about people like Jeffrey Dahmer doing things to animals, I think about how cruel it was of us to treat that cat that way.

Laura, Ohio was a quiet place without problems of pollution, crime and drugs. The largest business in town was a furniture store. It was a multi-building complex owned by Mr. Hobart Roark, who also served as a village mayor at one time. Mr. Roark had a very lovely wife and I found them to be very kind and helpful people who believed in God and had a small church that they helped start.

They had a huge neon sign over one of the

buildings that said in big red letters: "Jesus loves Roark Stores."

For a short time I even attended the little church that Mr. Roark established.

There were only two policemen in Laura that I ever knew of. The chief's name was Ross Netzley and his part time officer was Tom Todd. The chief was a rather large man, as far as weight goes and drove a fuel delivery truck, delivering heating oil and gas around the area. I believe that was his full-time job. He was a pretty stern looking man, but when encountering him I found him to be understanding and fair.

All the kids including myself respected him a great deal and were scared to death of him at the same time. The part time cop, Tom, was even bigger than the chief was. He was about six foot tall and weighed probably two hundred and sixty pounds, may be even more.

Now Tom was a lot of fun and we really liked him a lot. He used to chase us kids up and down the alleys because we would rattle the trash cans and run and hide from him. We would tell him that he could not find his butt with both hands because he was so big! Tom should have been a public relations man because he got along so well with us kids and our parents.

We made a bet with Tom one night at the Sinclair station that if he could not find us before we could get to him; he would buy us a chocolate shake. He agreed and we all took off to go hide.

I climbed out on this big limb that hung out over the sidewalk. I was getting tired and sore just waiting for him to come walking down the sidewalk. Boy was he surprised when I reached down and plucked his hat off his head and yelling "boo" as I did so. Seeing his face was worth the wait! You know; the guy actually took me to the Sinclair station and bought me a big chocolate shake. I'll never know what happened to Tom: the last I heard somebody said he passed away.

There was an old closed schoolhouse in town, and we used to play in the gymnasium. It still had the basketball hoop but we had to put new nets up. We played there all the time.

I can still remember Vernon going up in the belfry of the old bell tower to capture a screech owl. He took it home and put it in a cage. He later put his hand in the cage to feed or pet it, nobody knows for sure but he ended up going to the hospital to get his hand stitched up. That owl tore him up really bad!

When that happened, he was told by the game warden that by law he could not trap or cage the owl and he had to turn it loose. I guess it must have been an endangered species or something.

On Saturday nights we had a guy come to town and show free movies on the side of an old building. Boy was that great. My mom used to make us all a big bag of popcorn and we just had a great time.

I always hear a lot of children today saying "I'm bored" and wonder why these kids can't think of things to do to have fun without getting into trouble. What is wrong with the kids today is they have no imagination. They sit around playing high-tech games and never learn about reality.

I remember Gibbs Market. All the kids met there to catch the bus for school. We would spend our lunch money for pop and candy before we ever got on the school bus. We even talked about what we were going to do after the school day ended. We were never bored. There were so many fun things to do back then. We used our imaginations!

FIRST GIRLFRIEND

I still remember my first girlfriend. Her name was Susan. I know her last name but I will leave it out to protect the innocent. She was a cute little thing as I remember. I didn't remember what ever happened to her after I left school and joined the Army, but I have since learned that she married some guy, divorced and remarried again. I don't think she ever had any children of her own.

She and I had attended cotillion dance lessons together, went to football games and other school functions together, a lot of times. I still remember standing around at recess and holding hands out by the baseball dugouts. I also remember losing my virginity with her out in the milk parlor where her step dad had a farm.

I used to help her father with some of the farm chores on his dairy farm. It was a real nice farm just outside of Laura, Ohio. The farm sat on top of a hill with large barns and white fences around it. Her father also raised sheep, as I remember. I used to go to sales with him where he sold and bought sheep.

Her mother was a very nice lady who could make the best cookies and pies around. I can't remember ever going to the house that I didn't get cookies and milk. Sometimes I even had dinner with them.

I rode my Wizard motorbike about two miles to get to her house. It took quite awhile to get there, but it beat peddling a regular bike! Her mom and dad had been attending a farm sale one day and she got to stay home by herself. She called and invited me over. WHOA! What a trip that was!

That wizard motorbike was my very first motorized vehicle and it was a lot of fun. It was belt driven. You had to run alongside of it, jump on the seat and at the same time, release the compression lever so the motor would start.

In reality, it was a hell of a way to start a motor bike. If you missed the seat when you jumped on; there was a bar there that you would landed on, which would ring your bells real good!

I remember scaring the daylights out of my mother. We lived in Ludlow Falls, Ohio at the time. I had just attended a class picnic and was trying to get back home before I got soaking wet as it was already beginning to rain.

I went around a corner too fast and was really leaning into the curve when the tires let go of the pavement and started sliding across the street. When I hit the curb, the bike just flipped me right into the neighbor's yard!

Ludlow Falls, Ohio probably had a population of one or two thousand people. I can still remember well this quiet little town. It had one policeman who lived next door to our house. He was just a part-time policeman and was only stern when he had to be.

I remember the summer nights when it was nice and warm and about ten or twelve of us kids used to play "kick the can" under the streetlight. We played in front of the old firehouse. I do not ever recall an older person raising hell about us making noise or causing a ruckus. As a matter of fact, they would sit on their porch in the cool air of the evening and laugh while we played under the streetlight. Susan was always there cheering me on.

Every now and then someone would get hit by a flying can and stitches were required. Bats would fly around the street light at night. Some of the girls were scared, because, it was said that if a bat got in your hair, you would have to cut your hair off to get the bat untangled from it. I personally have never seen a bat in anyone's hair.

My brother Bill and I used to catch bats by tying a corncob on a four or five foot piece of kite string then tie it to an old cane fishing pole. We would swing the pole around in a circle under the streetlight and soon a bat would begin following it.

We would let the bat follow it for about fifteen or twenty rounds and then hit the ground with the corncob. The bat would do the same. Then we put the bat, if it was alive, in a metal box and take it home. We would scare the hell out of my sister and my mother. My mother would make us get that thing out of the house, raising her voice to a siren pitch! She was yelling something about being bitten and getting rabies or something worse!

We brought home other things besides bats. We would bring home snakes, owls, birds, dogs, cats, mice, hamsters, and even goldfish from the local county fair. The fish eventually ended up being flushed down the almighty throne!

In this same small town at Christmas time, thousands of people came to see the water falls. The falls was lit up with a zillion Christmas lights; which was an annual thing. The local volunteer fire department put all these lights up and decorated the falls. There was a manger scene with Jesus and other displays that included a Santa Clause, reindeer, snowmen, and other ornaments. The donations from the falls were used to purchase new equipment for the fire department. It was great time for our little town, but as time passed, the fire department quit having these events. The cost to fund this event was probably overwhelming.

Stupid is Stupid Does

I remember swimming in Ludlow Falls as a kid. The whole gang was down there and we always had a ball. The one event that I remember most was when Doris Johnson, the younger sister to my friend Richard Johnson, was with us and decided she wanted to swing on a rope we had tied to a tree.

This rope was at least one inch thick and would swing out over the gorge. The rope would probably swing out twenty feet or so over the water. Now everybody knew that it was a one way trip. You had to swing out, let go of the rope, and drop into the water. If you didn't let go, you would swing back into the side of the cliff that surrounded the gorge and probably kill yourself! Hmmm!

Doris, who was a tomboy and a petite type of girl, was insistent that swinging on the rope was going to be a fun thing to do.

Almost all the guys there who knew her disagreed. They told her it was too dangerous, that she would get scared and not let go of the rope. Doris's older brother Richard said, "Let her go for it." Richard felt she could do it and for us to leave her alone.

So I handed her the rope and said, “It’s your funeral, have at it!”

Doris took the rope, backed up as far as she could and launched herself into space! As she left the cliff top, I told her brother Richard, “She’s not going to let go of the rope!” We started yelling at her to let go of the rope. She apparently did not hear us yelling or was so damned scared she held onto the rope and swung back into the side of the cliff and fell into the rocks below!

After we got her out of the falls, news from the hospital was that she had a broken leg, broken collarbone, stitches over her eye, and numerous bruises.

After this incident, the rope was taken down. The village council was looking into different ways they could stop everyone from swimming in the gorge. While the council was busy with all the legalities, some crazy drunk person from Dayton, Ohio, decided he was going to jump off the cliff from the backside of the gorge. We local kids knew not to jump from that area because of a stone ledge just beneath the water. He nearly killed his fool self! The council put a screeching halt to the swimming at the Ludlow Falls gorge. We all missed being able to spend our summers there.

Dumb Things Kids Do

The fire department had a smoke machine that they used to fog the town to kill mosquitoes. They would drive around town billowing out a thick cloud of white smoke that contained some sort of insecticide that would kill these little blood suckers.

Naturally, one of the less intelligent guys in town decided to ride his bike in the smoke behind the application truck. The idiot finally got so sick; he fell off his bike in the middle of the street! I always said he was lucky it didn't kill him.

I still remember those mosquitoes; those dog gone things could bite like the dickens and leave bumps on you the size of a golf ball. I think they must have drunk a gallon of blood everyday from different people in town.

I had my first years of Scouting while living in the town of Ludlow Falls. While my experiences are many, only a few are still so fresh in my mind, it's as if they happened just a few hours ago.

We scouts were out playing in this large field that was in front of the scout masters home. We were throwing different things at each other, just having fun.

I don't know the name of the weed we were pulling up out of the ground, but when you cleaned the dirt off the roots, it looked like a spear.

We would throw these spears at each other. Talk about real stupidity! One of the guys, Jim Fetters, was hit on top of the head with one of these spears, causing a superficial cut. We lied to our scout master, telling him that Jim had fallen down and hit his head on an old board. We actually made the story believable by putting some blood on the corner of the board, (again proving that props can make most stories believable). Jim received a real chewing out by our Boy Scout master, when he found out how it really happened.

After putting a band-aid on Jim's head, we proceeded to do what most dumb kids do. We continued to play the same fool game we were playing before. Yes, you probably guessed it, another injury! The scoutmasters' son, Robert Widner, who is now deceased, got hit in the eye. His eye was severely injured. It almost cost him his eyesight and a close call with death.

What I remember most about Robert, was he always acted like he was hurt when we played around. He would fall down and roll around on the ground screaming like he was hurt. When all the guys would run to his aid, he would jump up and say "I fooled you!" like the old story of crying wolf.

Well, when Bobby got hit and started rolling around on the ground, everyone thought he was just fooling around again. When he stood up, we could see the blood coming from between his fingers. We knew then something was seriously wrong.

After this incident, the whole troop just kind of fell apart. Since Robert's dad was the scoutmaster, I imagine he was quite upset, to say the least, about the stupidity of the game we were playing.

I know Robert missed a lot of school that year. I can still remember, sometime in his junior or senior year, Bobby didn't wake up one morning. His mother found him deceased and I often wondered if it was possible that the previous eye injury somehow contributed to his death.

There was a large new bridge built almost directly over the gorge and falls where we used to swim. During the construction, Tom Shuff and I were playing around some big concrete tiles and culvert pipes when we uncovered a very large nest of bumblebees! I can still see Tom (in my thoughts), running like hell down over the hill with a small dark cloud of bees in hot pursuit. I think he only got stung a couple of times.

Although my dad wasn't one of us kids that hung around together, he acted like one of us and spent a lot of time with my friends and me. My dad was a great mechanic too. He was always fixing old cars and motorcycles.

He would take us kids for rides around town. I remember dad and my Uncle Oscar was working on an old motorcycle. Uncle Oscar was pulling the motorcycle that dad was seated on, with a piece of rope tied to the bike. They were trying to get it to start. Dad let out on the clutch, causing the bike to slide. Dad to hit the pavement with a thud and was drug about fifteen feet or so before Uncle Oscar realized what was happening.

My father was not seriously hurt as I recall, but he sure did get skinned up real good. He took a long time to heal up and hair over. I don't recall him ever getting onto any motorcycles after that! He still worked on them a lot though.

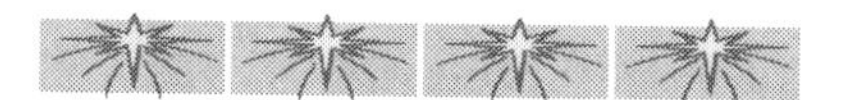

My oldest brother Bill got a motor scooter called a Salisbury. To be honest, it was the weirdest looking thing I had ever seen in my life. I just had to ride the ugly thing, and bugged my brother till he finally let me. He started it up for me, I jumped on it, and he turned me loose! I put the gas to it and it took off like a jet! I went between a pole and a barn where you could not walk through! I proceeded through the next door ladies flower garden before I got it under control! My brother Bill caught holy hell from dad for letting me ride the thing in the first place.

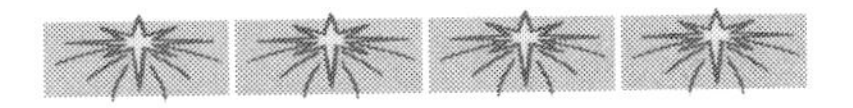

Blowing up the town

I remember catching hell for trying to blow the whole damn town up when I was messing around with some homemade gunpowder. It was some that my brother Bill and I had left over from a school fair project. The project was to make a volcano out of paper-mache. We had a tin can of some sort in the top of this homemade volcano. We took homemade gunpowder, put it in the tin can, and dropped a match in it. The gunpowder would spew up and make it look like a volcano was erupting. I did receive an honorable mention for the project.

I took the leftover gun powder home. While hiding behind a five hundred gallon propane fuel tank, I poured some gunpowder on the ground, and lit it. You could hear a very loud whoosh sound and see a huge plume of smoke!

While doing this stupid stunt, a small spark got into the coffee can that housed the remaining gunpowder. It went off with a loud boom shaking the house and earth!

I guess it must have scared the daylights out of my mother because she was at the back door in a flash, yelling, "Gary Don"!! My mother always called me that when she was upset, frightened, or really mad at me.

I peeked around the corner of the house to let her know I was still alive. She freaked out even more when she saw I had no hair or eyelashes on my face any longer. She said I looked like I was burned up really bad but in reality; it didn't burn me at all! All the white paint on the side of the tank had turned black! I don't think my dad had to mow that section of grass for the rest of the summer!

I received an Honorable Mention for my science project but that was a mere whisper compared to what I heard for the latter escapade, let alone the fear of gunpowder from that day on.

It wasn't too long after the gunpowder incident that my father bought a house in Laura, Ohio and we began the preparations for moving. Laura, Ohio was just a few miles up the road from Ludlow Falls.

The property my folks bought had an old shed on it that sat real close to the back of the house. There was an open cistern on the property and the place needed a lot of work. I still remember my Uncle Oscar coming over to help tear down that old shed. My father, my older brother and I began the task of repairing and remodeling the house so it could be lived in.

These were the things that my dad did all his life, repairing and fixing things to make life better for his family. These are the times when I learned a lot from my dad. I learned to do a lot of things on my own, but the basics were learnt from my dad. Later in life, I rebuilt and remodeled many homes and other buildings and hopefully, helped others in the process.

Helping my dad remodel this house was sometimes a dirty job. Plaster is dirty as hell, and carrying that stuff to the trash was always my job. It was a lot of hard work trying to make everything nice for us to live in.

The people who lived in that house before us had a bunch of dogs and left a large mess to be cleaned up. We tore down a bunch of dog houses and pens, and clean up piles of their messes. It took four or five days to clean that mess up but we made the back yard a place where you could actually enjoy sitting around and playing.

I made some new friends in this new town and was soon playing games with a couple of guys named, Dale and Vernon. We had some good times in Vernon's dad's barn. This was where we played basketball because his barn was the only place in town that had a basketball net. This old barn also had a large hayloft in it. Dale, Vernon and I used a large rope to swing from one hayloft to the other.

Like most kids, we had broken bones (that's another short story) from jumping out of the windows of that old barn, with umbrellas. I guess we thought we could fly! Not!!!!

Other good times included the go-carts down at the red bridge, at the foot of a large hill, just outside the village limits. Now, why they called it the "red bridge" is beyond me! I can never remember the bridge being any other color but silver!

Dale, Vernon, and I would build ramps on the hill and jump our bikes over them. Sometimes we would get our homemade carts and jump the ramps with those also.

Then we got this daredevil of an idea to jump over the ramps and through walls of fire! We built the walls in the road from straw we gathered from a nearby field. Hot damn! I don't think my mother knows yet to this day how my eyelashes and hair always seem to be burnt off!

The Town Bully

The little town had its share of bullies too. This particular fellow thought he could ride his bike over "our" ramps and show us little guys how "bad" he was. He didn't look very tough when they loaded him in the hearse and took him to the hospital. Back then, a hearse took you to the hospital, because there were no squad services.

I guess he just did not look to see how much loose gravel there was in the area where his bike had to land. His bike ended up in the dump or a junkyard, I suppose!

I recall another favorite pastime we had. We played rodeo at David's place. David, (another friend of mine), lived on a cow farm. We would ride the calves. Boy could those calves take off fast and stop even faster! We always ended up going head first into a fence or watering trough!

I can still remember the bully, Jerry, and I will refrain from using his last name to protect the stupid. I still remember him telling us little guys that he could ride a calf better than all of us and he was going to ride the biggest calf there!

We had built a gate system with a gate that swung open just like in the real rodeos. We hung a sign above the gate, with big white painted letters

(BAR C RANCH) on it. The sign hung so low that when entering or exiting through the gate, you had to duck your head. Now when Jerry jumped on that calf's back, that calf took off like a rocket! Jerry, not realizing how low the sign was, failed to duck! I recall David's dad, having to take Jerry to the doctor to get his face put back together. We never did have to worry about Jerry showing us how to ride a calf again!

Like most kids, I had my own paper route in Laura. I delivered the Journal Herald, a Dayton, Ohio newspaper. The paper had to be delivered before I went to school and for the most part, it was a lot of fun.

I could always tell when the weather was going to change. I remember when the old prop airplanes passed overhead. The sounds of the engines were very different when the weather was changing. It's a totally different sound with each type of weather. These sounds became very helpful to me when delivering newspapers. I know those sounds when I still hear them today.

I also learned back then that my feet did not like cold weather. They hurt so bad that I had to start on my deliveries about 3 a.m. to get my route done in time to get ready for school. My oldest brother used to help me sometimes (guess he felt sorry for me). We had a lot of fun together and always got done with the route in about half the time.

The only thing I really didn't like about the paper route was the fact that I had to collect money every Saturday from my customers. I think it was like twenty five or thirty cents a week! Sometimes I had to go back three or four times to collect such a meager amount and it would sometimes mess my whole day up. Well, if you had a job to do, you did it, no matter what!

Every Saturday, after collecting my profits from the paper route, I would save back money for Christmas. I caught the dickens and sometimes got grounded for a night or two because mom and dad thought I was blowing my money. When mom opened her Christmas gift Christmas morning, they were really sorry for disciplining me because I had bought my mother her very first fur coat! When mom opened that box and I saw her face, it was worth every minute of the hell I had caught. I still remember seeing the little tears in the corners of her eyes! That Christmas was just as awesome as mom was and still is!

MY FIRST AUTOMOBILE

I can still recall the first car I ever owned; it was a 1949 Pontiac coupe and had a flat head straight eight engine in it.

This car was a thing of beauty to me. It was a two door coupe, emerald green in color and did not have a scratch on it anywhere. It would really go fast if it had ten miles of road to wind up!

Owning this car taught me that, "you never talk back to your mother!" Mom had taken my car keys because I was late getting in and she decided that I could ride the bus home from school for a few days for punishment.

I was standing in front of the bathroom mirror, combing my duck style hair cut when I bad mouthed her by saying, "that was my damn car and I want my keys back!" Mom opened the door, slightly, and punched me in my mouth causing me to fall backward into the tub.

I paid for my Pontiac by working for my dad at his Texaco gas station and at the West Milton land fill. Dad had bought the local Texaco gas station in West Milton. Dad and I both ran this station for quite some time. My dad worked in Dayton, Ohio at Dayton Forge and Heat Treating during the day.

After school I would run the Texaco station and dad would run it when he got home from his day job.
It was around this time that my father got his foot crushed at the foundry. The injury was so bad that he had to quit the steel foundry, but he and I continued running the Texaco station.

I also worked at the landfill and dad and I would gather old refrigerators, stoves or any other kind of heavy metal that had any value.

Once a week a man would stop by and buy the old junk from us. He would try to talk us down to the lowest dollar he could. Dad knew how to get the best price, so the guy paid dad, loaded up his stuff and was on his way. Dad could bargain with the best of them!

Dad later closed the Texaco service station because the county was trying to force him to replace the underground tanks, claiming that they were leaking. Dad said the cost of replacing the tanks was more than the station was worth so dad closed it down and sold it.

After the sale of the Texaco station, I continued to work at the West Milton landfill. This job was an experience within itself.

Frank Howell, a friend of mine, would come down to the land fill. I would give him money, he would go to town for pop and snacks, and we would sit around looking at girly books that we found in other peoples trash.

After we got tired of the books, we began collecting every aerosol can we could find. We put them in a bushel basket till we had it overflowing. We gathered some old tires and placed them around the bushel basket. We set the tires on fire and it didn't take long until the place sounded like a war zone.

One time I remember the West Milton police came down to the landfill to find out if we had a machine gun! What a great time we had. It was later on in life when I realized just how dangerous that was! That stupid act could have harmed or killed a person if they would have gotten hit by them. Thank God that didn't happen!

My First Scooter

I can still remember the Cushman motor scooter I had. My friend Frank and I used to ride it all over the place.

We once rode it out to this girl's house. Frank and I would argue for ten minutes about who was going to "make out" with her first! Frank always seemed to win! He would climb through the window and after awhile: my turn would come. We would get back on the scooter and go back to the landfill where I was supposed to be working. Across the road from the landfill was a large thicket of woods and every Thursday we noticed that a woman would walk into the woods and disappear. Just a little while later, a man would do the same thing.

Frank and I watched this go on for a couple of weeks. We became curious (as young boys do) and quietly went into the woods after observing the man go in. Boy did we get an eyeful! These people were having a picnic on a blanket that they had spread on the ground. What happened next just knocked our socks off! They were having sex right there in the middle of woods!

They never knew they had an audience. We were tempted, many times, to jump out and yell "boo." We never did! I often wonder whatever happened to those people and who they were.

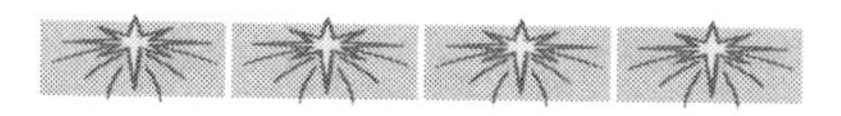

Going In The Service

School was great for awhile but I just got stupid and decided one day that I just did not want to go anymore. I talked my mom and dad into signing a letter stating that I was allowed to join the Army because I was quitting school.

I actually finished high school after joining the military thru the United States Army General Education Division. I actually graduated before my class did!

I went to the recruiting station in Piqua, Ohio and talked to a recruiter. The officer told me and my friend Gail Davis, that if we joined the service together, we would be joining on the Buddy plan. This meant that we would be guaranteed to stay together through basic training. After basic training, we possibly could stay together during schooling if we chose the same courses at A.I.T, (advanced infantry training), or the Signal Corps. This was when I found out you could not trust anything the military told you.

Gail and I went to Fort Thomas, Kentucky on Feb. 19, 1960, raised our right hand and swore to defend the interest and people of the United States and the Constitution there of. We were loaded on a bus to be transported to our base for basic training.

After getting on the bus I started looking for my friend. I knew something was wrong when I realized he was not on that bus.

It was the last time I ever remember seeing my friend. I found out later, he was sent to Fort Benjamin Harrison, In. and I was sent to Fort Knox, Ky. for basic training.

I arrived at Fort Knox, Ky. on February 24th, 1960 and was assigned to ACo 1stBn 6thArmd Cav for nine weeks of basic training. I liked basic training because I enjoyed marching and crawling in the mud. I remember it being very cold because it was early March.

I remember an African-American guy by the name of Hereford, who was in my company. He seemed to be able to sleep anywhere at any time. We found him sleeping on the john (toilet) once, so we dumped a bucket of water on him! Damned if that didn't wake him up!

I found that there were guys from all over the country in my unit with me and almost every one of them got along really great. We all were on a long march and came to a hill that was called "agony" and for good reason too! The hill was steep as hell and covered with ice and snow on this particular day. This red headed guy from

Kansas, who was only five foot three or so, fell. He was crawling on his belly and elbows trying to get up that hill. A guy by the name of Terry M. offered to carry his weapon for him. Terry was politely told to "back off" because nobody carries their weapon but themselves. This guy was one tough man who ended up getting a ribbon for his stamina and guts.

Basic training was nothing but a bunch of running your butt off. We had to run double time everywhere we went. I don't know why we ran double time, because we arrived earlier than we were supposed to. Because we were early, we had to wait in the damn cold for fifteen or twenty minutes to get in the building. I remember a sergeant by the name of Benicia. He was a heavy set man, who just could not keep up with the rest of us. When we would run double time, he always had us go slow, taking half steps. He still had a tough time keeping up, but, he was really a great sergeant.

Our platoon Sergeant, I believe is name was Miller, was of German descent. Miller was really strict and did a great job as a drill instructor.

I personally believe he wanted us to think he was strict just to make us dislike him. I do remember him hitting a recruit on top of his steel pot (helmet) with a flashlight when he got out of step during a march.

I remember having to hold my weapon over my head and run double time around the whole platoon (while they were marching straight time,) because I got out of step with the rest of them. I also remember guys carrying bricks around all day in their right or left hand because they got out of step while marching to the mess hall or some other location.

After basic training was completed in April of that year, my conduct and efficiency were both rated excellent!

I just wanted to go to advanced infantry training and become a drill instructor. Again, the Army, through their magical information system, decided that I had no clue as to what I wanted to do. I was allowed to take a two week leave to go home. When I returned to base, I was prepared for my next assignment. I was sent to Fort Gordon, Georgia on the 13th of May, 1960, to be trained as a secret agent in StuCoC USASTR 11-6600-03. The Army tried to teach me to type something called crypt! All my life I had no ambition to type and the only reason I took typing in school was because the teacher was good looking. I really didn't like typing crypt, so I requested to be transferred out of that unit.

On June 26th, I was transferred to another unit on the same base. In this unit, I was a telephone lineman. I learned to climb poles, repair electric lines, and run and repair large diesel generators. These generators provided emergency power to large buildings like a hospital or factory. I was still in the signal Corps but it was in a different location.

I completed the schooling for that assignment in Sept 1960 and my conduct and efficiency was rated "excellent", again.

Next, I was transferred to a small Nike missile base in Pedricktown, New Jersey. I arrived there Sept, 3rd 1960 and was assigned to the 56th Signal Detachment.

I soon found out that there was not even a job on the base for my MOS. I was stuck as a gate guard or I was on KP (kitchen patrol) all the time. I began complaining that this place did not have a job that called for my MOS 624. In guess my complaining worked because I was transferred to B Battery 3rd Missile Battalion 60th Artillery in Warrington, Pa... Again I was rated with an excellent rating in both conduct and efficiency.

My understanding that the military would be an opportunity for change did not work to my benefit. I began creating problems by simply not following orders, like not getting out of bed. In

November 1960, I failed to fall out for the morning muster and got an article fifteen. I was restricted to the IFC (launch area) of the base. I went to the major's office during this time and told him I just wanted out of the service if they could not find a location that suited me for what I was trained for. To make my point clear, I took a slug of Aqua Velva after shave, and told him I would be leaving the damn place one way or another and left his office!

I received a summary court-martial for "disrespect to an officer" and for "breaking restriction" because I came to his office from the launcher control area without permission. I was found not guilty of the first offense, and guilty of the second. I forfeited twenty five dollars of my one hundred dollar pay for that month.

I was transferred to Battery A 2nd missile Battalion 59th Artillery which was the same unit but in a different area of the base. They gave me a military driver's license and assigned me to hauling all the bases' laundry to Valley Forge, Pa... I would pick up the preceding weeks laundry and head off back to base.

I found out I could "move off" base if I was married. I started hanging out in places where I could meet a decent girl.

I actually began having a good time and liked

driving the truck hauling laundry during the day.

Everything seemed to be going well for me, for a change!

Myself and a couple of other guy's from the base started going to this skating rink. It was a great place to blow off steam and meet girls!

A funny story comes to mind and I just have to tell it. Three guys and I were at the rink having a great time. Just before we arrived at the rink, we had consumed some beer while riding around. Steve was feeling really good and going around the rink floor very fast.

The rink had a side door that they kept opened for fresh air. The doorway had a 2 X 4 across the opening to keep anyone from going out. Steve, who was half drunk, could not get stopped and did a flip right over the 2X4. He landed on his rear, outside of the building. We received a stern warning that "any further horseplay and we would be thrown out of the place."

MY FIRST WIFE

I met a young woman at the skating rink and we began seeing each other most weekends. After dating her for a while, I felt this was the woman that I wanted to marry. She was from Oreland, Pa. and had a couple of sisters and a nice home. I met her mom and dad and we got along great at first. Her dad fancied himself as an inventor and was always showing me things he thought were great ideas. Of course, I always agreed even though I thought some of his ideas were pretty stupid.

I ask her to marry me and we were married on April 15, 1961. Keeping in mind I wanted to live off base, I hurriedly went back to the base and showed my base commander my marriage certificate! I was allowed to move off base! I knew in my subconscious all this was happening because I just wanted to get off the base.

My new wife and I moved into a small house trailer in Pottstown, Pa... We started out pretty good with the help of her folks. The Army gave us a forty dollar per month living quarter's allowance.

I continued to drive the truck back and forth to Valley Forge, Pa. and was having a great time. As luck would have it, I screwed up again.

On July 11, 1961, Steve Walker and I were on our way back to the base when a guy and his wife came up alongside the laundry truck I was driving and blew the horn, waving for us to pull over. I had no clue who this guy was. He was in civilian clothes and I was not going to pull over for him or anyone else. I sped up to try and get away from him and he finally gave up the chase.

We got back to the base and just went about our normal routines. But alas! The ordeal was not over! I got called to the company commanders' office and on the 13th of July, I got another Article fifteen. I lost my military drivers license and had to do two hours of extra duty for fourteen days. I ended up on KP duty or guard duty again! I found out later, the guy in the car was a Major from Ft. Dix, New Jersey.

I was so pissed off that I just stayed in bed and did not report for formation or KP duty. I received another Article fifteen and was restricted again to the base for fourteen days. This time that Article fifteen kept me from getting to go home for Christmas! I was really mad!

I guess things were just going to get worse from that point on because I did not care if I **ever** followed another order from anyone else. So, on Jan 22, 1962 I again refused to go to formation and to KP duty. I received my last OFFICIAL reprimand!

Later that month, I asked the major for a transfer or

to just let me out of the military. The major asked me "on what grounds?" I told him I did not care what grounds he used, I just wanted out!

It was later that month that I was called to the COs office. He informed me that I was being discharged from the military with a general discharge under honorable conditions. He said I would be transferred to Fort Dix, New Jersey to muster out.

I was truly happy about this at the time, because I knew I was getting out. My CO requested I go do my duties as a gate guard until my final orders came. I happily agreed, and for once I actually enjoyed myself. On the evening of May 16, 1962, the night before I was transferred to Ft Dix, I was approached by a sergeant, whom I previously had problems with. I did not like him nor did he like me. I was a smart ass at the time and refused to take any crap from his stripes.

It was late that night, sometime after midnight, when he showed up at my post. He proceeded to tell me that he came down there for the sole purpose of kicking my butt. I, not wanting to create a problem that could possibly interfere with my transfer out of the military, politely told him that he was "incapable of that task." I told him that he was really stupid for making a statement like that to a guy who did not like him, was armed with a firearm, and was thought to be crazy by most people on base.

I quickly jacked a round in the chamber of my firearm and politely told him he had ten seconds to get his butt back to the barracks. I started counting to ten. The last time I saw him, he was going through the door of the barracks, which was about one hundred twenty yards away. I swear he made the hundred yard dash in less than ten seconds!

Shortly thereafter, I transferred to Fort Dix New Jersey where I was mustered out of the service and received my general discharge under honorable conditions.

I had to turn in all of the equipment that was issued to me by the United States Army. I was only allowed to keep the things that I had purchased during my military stint, like, extra T-shirts, khakis, hats, and such. My military time amounted to about two years and three months.

After I received my papers, I walked out of the gate there at Fort Dix and politely took the duffel bag that I had, laid it on the ground, struck a match and set it on fire. In hindsight, I wish I hadn't burned it, but that's just the way my mentality was at that time. I was just so mad and upset that the military had absolutely jerked me around from the time I got in, until the day I got out.

Even on my last day, the MPs actually came out the gate and tried to tell me that I could be arrested for destroying military property. I showed the MP my orders, and that he had no jurisdiction over my burning my own personnel property. I told him that I could do as I damn well pleased with it! The MP went back to his guard house and left me alone.

Nowadays, if you did that act in town, they would probably arrest you for open burning or maybe you'd be cited for burning refuge in the city limits. But, in 1962 there was no law like that that I knew of.

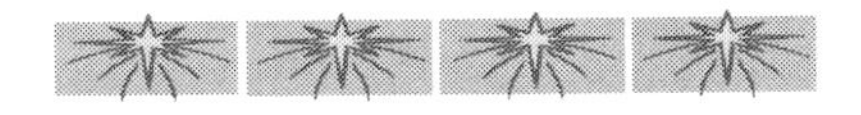

Civilian Again

After I had gotten out of the Army at Fort Dix, New Jersey, my wife and I had moved into a small house trailer in Pottstown, Pa... We both began looking for work. Her mother was able to get her on where she worked, making pretty good money. I found a job working at a gas station as a mechanic and an all around cleanup person. Civilian life was beginning to look good again.

I had met and served in the army with a guy by the name of Steve Walker. Steve was a tall, lanky kind of guy, with greasy hair and a ruddy complexion. He hailed from the state of Washington. Steve had gotten out of the service just shortly after I did, maybe two or three months later.

Steve had bought a 1949 Ford from some gentlemen around Doylestown, Pennsylvania. His intentions were to drive the car back to his home, but changed his mind and decided to fly back instead. Steve offered to sell the car to me for 50.00. I paid him for the car, and then found out why he decided to get rid of it so quickly. The car had a spun rod bearing and it started knocking like hell soon thereafter.

I took the car to my father-in-laws home where there was a garage to work on it. I started working on it by removing the oil pan and looking for the bearing that was bad.

A few days later, I was at home messing around when there was a knock at the door. I opened the door and there stood Chuck Wright, another army friend of mine. I invited him into the trailer. A big blond headed guy and another fellow, whom I did not know, followed Chuck into my trailer. The blonde headed guy claimed that Steve had gotten the car from him and failed to pay for it. He wanted the car back!

By this time, Steve was already back in Seattle, Washington. I told the guy I had paid Steve for the car and he was welcome to take it as long as he paid me back the purchase price!

The blonde guy proceeded to tell me they were going to take the car. I told him I had a bill of sale and the car title was in my name.

He advised me that he was going to kick my butt if I did not give him the car. This is when I was thinking Chuck would be on my side to even out the odds! I opened my big mouth and proceeded to tell him that the car was going to remain right where it was unless he had my fifty dollars!

They, (including Chuck) proceeded to kick the crap out of me, in my own trailer! I still remember being dumbfounded knowing that Chuck was taking part in this deal. Chuck and the other guy were not that much bigger than me. On the other hand, this blonde haired fellow was huge! He kept trying to break a soda bottle on the edge of my sink. Back then, the kitchen sink area in house trailers had a metal strip going around the face of the countertop. He had that metal strip absolutely torn off the side of the countertop!

He kept saying he was going to "cut me up" and probably would have if that bottle had broken! Instead, they just kicked the crap out of me and said they'd be back and I better have the car there. Now I, being the lawful owner of the car, and the smart ass that I was, continued looking for the chance to get even.

Revenge Is Sweet

About a month or so later, I was walking down the street; I believe it was in Doylestown or Pottstown, Pennsylvania. I had seen this blonde headed fellow and recognized him walking down the street in front of me.

I only weighed about one hundred sixty pounds at the time, so I knew I would only have one shot at getting even. I took off on a dead run, and ran as hard as I could run. When I came up behind this blonde headed guy, I hit him right in the back of the head, with my fist, as hard as I could and kept on running like the wind! I knew that he would kick my butt if he saw me. I thought it was chicken shit of me to sucker punch him that way, but three against one was chicken shit too, don't you think?

As I rounded the corner, I looked back and saw him sprawled out on the sidewalk. I don't know how bad he was hurt, and I never stopped to find out. At the time, I doubt the fellow had no clue who hit him as I never seen him again. He should have remembered later because I told him that I would get even! I figured he must not have died since I didn't read anything in the papers about it.

There was a knock on my trailer door about three weeks later.

Whoever it was was pounding on the door as if to say, "You better open the door or I'll kick it in!" I peeked out the window and saw that it was the "other guy" who had been with the blonde headed guy.

Now to get into my trailer, you have to climb up a few steps. This was an advantage point for me! I opened the door of the trailer and immediately kicked this guy right in the face as hard as I could kick. I jumped out of the trailer onto the top of his chest.

I can still remember him being hauled off by somebody in a car and I never seen him or the blonde headed guy ever again in my life! I did however; get a visit about a week later from Chuck.

He knocked on my door, backed up from the trailer a few feet and stood there until I opened the door. I said to him "what do you want?" He proceeded to apologize and tell me that he was sorry for his part in the altercation. The other two guys had led him to believe that the car was stolen. He said he had no idea that I had bought the car. Chuck thought they had told him the truth and had brought him to my place to help in retrieving the car.

I accepted his apology and he and I actually became pretty close friends after that.

Back Home to Ohio

Shortly after the Doylestown, Pa. incidents, my folks came from Ohio for a visit. Parents just seem to know when their children need them. Again, my mom and dad were there for me, in my time of need. My dad helped me put the new rod bearings in the engine and got it to running pretty good. I drove the car around town for a couple of days to make sure it could make the trip to Ohio. We loaded about everything we owned, in and on top of the car and headed out for the great state of Ohio.

On the way back to Ohio, (we were somewhere near Pittsburg, Pennsylvania), my father was driving, when a bee managed to fly in the window. The bee began buzzing around Larry Dean's (my little brother) head and he started yelling and screaming.

My dad tried to get the bee to go back out of the window and in doing so, he took his eyes off the road for just a second and rear ended another car. Everything that was on top of the car came off and landed on top of the hood. What a mess! Again, just something else in my life to go wrong! Well, we packed everything up and put it back on top of the car except for the baby bed. It was broken all to pieces, so we tossed it in the ditch, laughed it off as a bad dream and continued on to Ohio.

After arriving back in Ohio with the help of my folks, my wife, daughter and I settled into a small apartment in Potsdam, Ohio near where my folks lived. I began looking for a job but could only find work pumping gas.

I recall my wife being a real pain in the "you-know-what." All she wanted to do was watch soap operas and she did her level best to live the life of the actress's. She ran up the phone bill to the tune of hundreds of dollars, calling her mother back in Pa. and talking for hours at a time.

My mom, being the kind person she was, was doing all she could to help take care of our daughter while I worked. My wife also looked for work but spent most of the day watching the soaps.

The wife finally found a job as a waitress and did pretty well with wages and tips. Our credit was good and we were able to buy some decent furniture to help turn our apartment into a home. On Saturday evenings, my father and I also went to Joe's auction barn and bought items for our home.

As I continued working, I also was looking for a better paying job. I got a job at Uhlmans Department Store in Troy, Ohio. I unloaded trucks, stocked shelves and did general cleaning. I was making more money because I was getting more hours.

The fact that I was making more money allowed me

to move my family into a nicer apartment in Troy, Ohio. It was much closer to where my wife worked and even closer to my work. I even walked to work when the weather allowed it.

Bad company corrupts good character.

Menander

BAD COMPANY

While working at Uhlmans, I met a co-worker by the name of Jerry. He was a wiry character to say the least and was always looking for a way to make a fast buck, legally or not. He was a small fellow, about one hundred forty pounds and about 5’ 8” tall. I remember him having a burr hair cut and having a couple of missing teeth. In the twentieth century he would probably be called a neo Nazi. Of course, he wasn’t one though!

Jerry later introduced me to Paul, an older man in his sixties. I said “older” because at the time, sixty was “old” to me! This guy was tall and thin, always had a stubble for whiskers, and smelled like he worked on a pig farm!

Paul really did own a large farm on the outskirts of Troy but it was a cow farm. I used to go to his house and help him clean out the barns and feed a couple of steers that he was getting ready to butcher. I was supposed to get part of the meat for my pay but that never happened!

Paul was always talking about some plan to rob a bank or pull off other stupid stunts. I think he fancied himself as a modern day Al Capone. Paul was probably thirty or thirty five years older than Jerry and I and felt he could talk us younger ones into anything!

Oh, don't think I'm trying to lay blame on someone else for my stupidity, because I and I alone were responsible for my own wrongdoings. While playing cards at the farm one evening, Paul was talking about this retired postal worker who supposedly had hundreds of dollars hid away in his house and how easy it would be to get it.

Jerry, being the guy he was and always looking to impress Paul, jumped right on the wagon and started laying out plans on how to get into this guy's house and rob him. And yes, I, being stupid, and wanted to get hold of some "fast cash," went along with the plan.

Paul seemed to know when this retired guy got his monthly check and figured that would be the best time to rob him.

I cannot remember the date but I know it was very cold outside when Jerry and I knocked on the door of this elderly mans house. When he answered the door that was the first time I saw how bad Jerry really was.

As this event comes to mind, (what little memory I have left of it) it was late 1962. In 1962 I don't think there was a law on the books called, "home invasion" but that is exactly what it would be today.

Jerry proceeded to push this elderly gentleman around threatening to kick his butt if he did not tell him where the money was. The elderly man finally told Jerry where the money was while I pulled the phone wires from the wall. Jerry gathered the money up. We left without physically hurting the guy and jumped into Paul's pickup truck and left the area.

They dropped me off at my house after we agreed that Jerry would bring my cut to work the next day. This just goes to show how stupid I was. I had no clue how much money we even got in the heist. Jerry gave me twelve dollars and said that was my part. Do you believe it? All that stupidity and taking a chance on hurting someone for twelve lousy dollars! I still thank God to this day that this did not end any worse than it did.

I still believe that Jerry and Paul probably got a big laugh at how they were able to screw me out of my share. I'm sure they both got more than they said, but I guess that knowledge went to their graves with them. The last I heard, they were both deceased.

Not too long after we robbed the elderly man, Jerry and I were out late just driving around. There had been a snowstorm and we were spinning donuts in parking lots around town. We drove in front of a bar that sat along old Rt. 25 just on the outskirts of Troy, Ohio.

The bar was closed at the time because it was three thirty in the morning. Outside was dark as hell and as equally cold. I think the name of the place was the Diamond Club. Not quite sure.

We decided to go to the bar to get some booze and maybe even find some hidden money. So I turned the car around and drove past the place a couple of times to make sure it was indeed empty. We parked the car a short distance up the road and walked back to the place. I still recall freezing my butt off as we walked up the road in the slush and wet snow.

The front door was enclosed in a small entry way that gave us cover from passing traffic. We took a crowbar and broke through the door of the place. The door latch came apart very easy and we were able to walk in undetected. Jerry started looking for money while I took some bottles of liquor and a couple cartons of cigarettes. Jerry also grabbed some booze and cigarettes and we took off for the car.

We then took the stuff to Paul's house and proceeded to tell Paul about our escapade and how easy it was. Again Jerry said all he found was thirty dollars and gave me what he said was my share, a whopping ten dollars.

I started raising hell because I did not think Paul should get any of the cut for sitting on his butt while we did the deed, freezing our butts off in the cold. To settle the dispute, they gave me another five dollars, a carton of smokes, and a bottle of liquor. I took the stuff home and gave the wife all the cash. I told her that I had helped Paul at the farm.

Looking back, I realize now that I was on the wrong path with my life and most of all with God. I was too blind to see it. Even now, I sit and wonder how I could have been so stupid.

Now when I think back, I realize how God was watching over us and did not allow Jerry to actually harm anyone. I shudder to think where I would be today if someone would have been killed. I see young guys today making the same mistakes in their lives. I just wish I could talk to them, find out why they are in the fix their in and how I could help them out.

The wife and I both were working but still struggling from week to week to keep up with the bills and such. When I think about it, it would have been so much easier if I would have just stayed home and found a part time job. Anything would have been better than what we did!

It was the winter of 1962 to 1963 and getting close to Christmas. I had laid low for a while because the "break in" had actually scared me a bit. The argument over the money had really pissed me off at Jerry and Paul.

I continued working at the department store and really liked the job. I was stocking shelves and unloading trucks and just doing anything that my boss asks me to do. He was a great guy and a lot of fun to work with.

One day while we were working, my boss got a call advising him that his apartment was on fire. He loaded us guys into his car and we drove over to his place. On the way to his home, he kept saying that his art was all going to be ruined and he had to try and save it.

When we arrived, we found out that it wasn't his place that was on fire. It was his neighbor's house. Everything was cool at his house, so we went back to the store and continued working as usual.

Brownies Market

Sometime in early January 1963 Jerry and I met up with Paul at his farm. He told that he had this great caper all figured out and we could each get a couple thousand bucks. He knew of this place that supposedly always had four or five thousand dollars on hand and would be easy pickings. The worst thing about this place was that it was near the town where I grew up and I knew the owners. I told Paul that I had never heard of these folks ever having any money but then I had no clue as to their financial well being. I wonder even today just how Paul ever got this big story or if it was just a big lie on his part.

Jerry, Paul, and I went to this little gas station that was owned by an older couple. The little station was on the outskirts of a little town where I spent about ten years of my life. We drove by to see if any customers or other people were around. We did not see anyone, so Paul, who was driving my car, parked on a road that ran behind the place. Paul was to wait for Jerry and me and keep an eye open for the cops.

Jerry and I got out of the car. We walked across a gulley; a large field covered in snow and slush, and snuck up to the back of Brownies Market. We put our ski masks on, which felt pretty good, but only because it was so cold out there.

Jerry and I went into the front door with our masks on. Jerry, who had the firearm, pointed it at the older couple and said "this was a stickup." We robbed the older couple of what was in the register and tried to get them to give up the cash that Paul seemed to think they had hid someplace. Jerry actually threatened to shoot the older man if he did not tell us where all the money was. The old guy said "what you have is all there was." So we left.

After we left the place with about fifty dollars or so, we had to cross back over that field. While jumping over the gulley, I fell on my face hitting a rock and splitting my lower lip so bad that I had to go get stitches.

While I was getting my face put back together at the local hospital, Jerry and Paul divided up the money and I ended up with seventeen dollars and knew then that crime just did not pay at all!

When I got home, the wife wanted to know what happen to my mouth! I told her that I was helping Paul move a TV and tripped over something. I fell backwards allowing the TV to hit me in the mouth.

While I try to recall as much of my past as I can, it truly makes my stomach turn horribly sick. If and when this story is ever written and published, I wonder how much ridicule I will receive, how many friends I will lose, and possibly lose my family.

My family has not a clue as to all the problems I

have encountered through the years, as a result of my stupid actions.

As I mentioned earlier in this book, I just feel at this time in my life, I might be able to steer another young person to find better things to do with their life. I want to let others know that you can overcome the worst that life can offer with just a little common sense and a lot of good honest work.

On the Lam

It was a very short time after the incident at Brownies when Jerry got word that the police were looking for him. He came to my house saying, "We need to get out of town." We took off for Kentucky where Jerry had some relatives. It was a place where we could hide out for a while and let things cool off.

We got as far as southern Ohio into Scioto County when the car began to overheat. The heater did not work either. I later learned that I had failed to put antifreeze in the car to keep it from freezing up in the winter. I should have known better than this because I'm sure my father had taught me differently!

We continued traveling south and getting colder by the minute. We passed an old country store that looked like it was closed. We turned the car around to go back and see. We needed to find some water or antifreeze for the car and some warm clothes for ourselves! We drove by the store real slow and Jerry threw a rock through the window! He wanted to see if anyone would hear anything and come to investigate.

We waited for about half an hour and no one ever showed up. We went to the front door and broke in through it. We found some bib overalls and jackets. We put them on for warmth and continued to look for antifreeze.

We did find some candy bars and crackers to snack on so we gathered them up, closed the door and left.

We drove to Olive Hill, Ky. and a short time later the car finally gave it up and just quit. We decided to walk back to a small town we had just passed through. After walking for what seemed to be hours, we decided to find a place to get warm.

After slogging around for what seemed like two hours, we came upon an old barn that we could get into without breaking in. This barn had a large hayloft in it. We took bales of hay and built a small like cave to burrow into for warmth. We covered it with a tarp that we had found lying around. We crawled into the little cave, covered up, and actually slept till about 8:30 the next morning!

When we woke up, it was colder than an Eskimo well digger and we were hungry. We had already eaten all of the candy bars and crackers that we got from the old store the night before. We knew we had to get moving or we were going to freeze to death!

The barn was a good half mile off the road so we had to hoof it through a couple of snow drifts to get back to the road. Daylight was breaking so we decided to look for a house where we could get some water or anti-freeze for the car. After trudging through the snow and cold for about three hours, we came upon a guy who was cutting logs. He was trying to get the logs to his little house on the side of the mountain.

The guy would have his big old jack mule drag the logs down the hill and he would cut them up for firewood to heat his house. Jerry and I helped him out for two or three hours until the guy decided to quit for the day.

He invited us in for supper and it was one of the greatest meals I ever had in my life. Maybe it just seemed that way because I was famished by that time.

After dinner we sat around and talked for awhile. I told him about the car freezing up and quitting on us. He said he remembered seeing the car alongside the road and wondered who it belonged to. He agreed to bring the car to his house the next day and told us we could stay at his place for the night. His wife was a very nice lady. She fixed us a bed to sleep in and we slept better than we had in three days!

The next morning, the lady had fixed a breakfast fit for a king! We ate until we could eat no more! After breakfast we prepared to go get the car. It was amazing how close the damn thing was to where we were staying! How we missed the place I'll never know!

The guy brought his jack mule and a chain. I wouldn't have believed it if I had not seen it with my own eyes! That mule pulled that car like it was a toy, all the way back to the house. Upon close inspection, we found that the engine had a cracked block. That was the end of that car! I gave the car to the guy for all his troubles and thanked him for him and his family's help and hospitality.

The guy told us where the next little town was and we could hitch a ride from there. Since we did not have a car, we decided to go back to Ohio. We hitched a ride and got back to Ohio by the next day. It was just a couple of days after my birthday in 1963 and I was glad to be back in Ohio!

I remember it well. Ohio was cold and snowy, just like every winter is! My wife was glad to see me home and that I was ok. I guess she worried about me a lot. I told her I was going to get a new job and I was finished screwing around! I promised that I would not get into anymore trouble that would, land me in jail or even worse, get me killed! Little did I know that I was going to get help in that direction sooner than I thought!

IN CUSTODY

I'm really not sure of the exact date, but a knock came at my door. When I answered the door, my life truly went into total darkness. There stood the local police, who arrested and charged me with armed robbery. I was transported to the Miami County jail in Troy, Ohio to await trail.

Boy- oh- boy, what a change my life had taken! I was scared to death! It was not the first time I had been in jail. I had been arrested in Pennsylvania for "disturbing the peace." I spent five days in the county jail, but that is another time and story. Being put in handcuffs was a totally new experience for me and I did not like it! I knew then that it was not ever going to happen again!

I had no money, so the courts appointed me an attorney. His name was John Faulkner. I thought he was a good attorney and I believed him when he told me that it would be in my best interest to cooperate with the prosecutor's office. I was told to tell them everything they wanted to know, in reference to what Paul, Jerry and I had been involved in.

I arrived at the court house. Paul and Jerry were already there for our arraignment and the judge had set our bail. Paul was released on bail after putting up his farm to cover the bail but Jerry and I remained in jail.

After Paul got out of jail, he hired a big time lawyer and pled "not guilty" to all charges. Paul claimed he had nothing to do with what we all were charged with. He said he was not even with us during the robberies. Paul said Jerry and I did all of these crimes on our own. He tried to claim he did not even know me other than he knew I was Jerry's friend. This was the time in my life that I learned you have to know who your friends are and not to trust anyone!

When Jerry and I found out that Paul was going to blame everything on us, we decided to tell all. I ask to see my attorney. A couple of days later he came to see me. I cut a deal that I would plead guilty and would testify against both Paul and Jerry. The prosecutor told my lawyer that he would recommend leniency but could not promise any favors on sentencing.

I got word later that Paul was going to help Jerry get a good lawyer who could get him out on bail, if he would not go against him in the trial. This is when they separated Jerry and me so we could not talk to each other.

I found out much later, after my release, Jerry and I were separated in order to protect me. The prosecutor's office had heard someone say that they were going to get me or kill me. I guess Paul thought if I was dead, so was the case against him and Jerry.

Jerry went to trial first and copped a guilty plea for a shorter sentence. Jerry did testify against Paul at his trial because Paul failed to keep his word to Jerry. Paul did not get him a good lawyer nor did he get Jerry out on bail. I wonder if Jerry learned the same lesson I did about who your friends are.

Jerry was a short tempered guy. If you messed with him or his family, he would "get even." It may take him a while but he would eventually "get even." I remember a guy that failed pay back some money that Jerry had loaned him. Jerry ran into him on the street and cut the guy up really bad with a chain, that had razor blades attached to it. I should have ended our friendship right then and there!

I testified against Paul at his trial. I can still remember when he went to prison. Word was that when he got out of prison, I was a dead man! Even if I had gone to prison, it would not have been the same one that Paul had been sent to because to our age difference. I heard later on in life that Paul died while in prison.

I went back to court for sentencing. As I recall, I was the first person in the history of Miami County, to receive probation for the crimes that I had been charged with. My mother and father were there for moral support. I am so thankful, to this day, for the compassion the court showed towards me that day. It changed my life forever.

I still remember how scared I was when the judge said the words ten to twenty five years! He paused, to let it sink in for a bit, and then said he was suspending the sentence and placing me on probation for five years.

The court then read a list of rules I had to abide by. I was also required to get a job, pay restitution, and report to my probation officer once a week or any other times established by the probation department.

The judge then released me to the probation officer. I was taken to the county jail to retrieve what belongings I had there. They led me outside to where I got in my mom and dad's car to go home. It felt weird riding in a car after sitting in jail for three months or so.

Starting Over

We arrived at my folk's house in Potsdam, Ohio and after three months in the county jail, it was like a big classy hotel. My wife, daughter, and I were starting over as a family. To comply with my probation rules, I had to get a job. I took a job hanging and finishing drywall with Mueller Drywall Contractors out of West Milton, Ohio.

The guy who owned the company was Jim Mueller. He was from West Milton, Ohio and an employer I really enjoyed working for. He taught me a lot.

It was my understanding Jim had cancer and had to go through radiation treatments. I still remember he had a large burn place on his stomach from these treatments. I don't know whatever happened to him. He had a son who was a great kid and a wife who was very nice. The whole family was just great people. During the time I worked for Jim, he and I went to scuba diving school together. Classes were held at the YMCA in Piqua, Ohio. I got certified as a scuba diver. Jim and I dove in many different places around the states of Ohio and Indiana.

We went diving in an old stone quarry in the town of New Paris, Ohio. At that time, the quarry was called France Lake. It has since become a campground and now called, Natural Springs Resort.

I continued working for Jim. It did not take me long to learn the trade. Before I knew it, I was drywalling houses on my own that Jim had contracted. Jim felt I was trustworthy enough to be left alone to do the job right. I did not let him down. He was pleased with my work.

My wife and I were not getting along because she wanted more in life than I could provide at the time. She didn't seem to understand that I had to pay back restitution and court costs for awhile. I also had to report to my probation officer, which took that much more time and expense.

The wife would call her mother every day, creating large phone bills that we could not afford to pay. I had the phone taken out! That didn't stop her!

I found that she was using the next door neighbor's phone! I told the neighbor that I could not pay their phone bill and ask them not to let her use the phone unless it was an emergency. Boy did that make her mad!

I guess that was the straw that broke the camel's back because she said she wanted to move back to her mother's. She took our daughter and went back to her mom's.

Thirty More Days

About two years into my probation I met a guy from Troy, Ohio. I believe his first name was Frank but for the life of me I can't remember his last name. But, we started hanging around together, just working on cars, and chasing women.

We were in Dayton, Ohio on a Friday night and Frank said he was just about out of money and he knew how to get some fast cash. I should have known then that it was probably something illegal but it just did not come up in my thought process.

Now Frank was just a little guy about 5' 5' and maybe one hundred thirty pounds soaking wet. Frank had a very deep baritone voice that could be heard for blocks.

He asks me to drop him off at the Greyhound bus station because he was going to get him a gay person. In the early 60's that is what they called a guy who had sex with another guy. Nowadays that would be a horrible thing to say! I thought he was going to let the guy play with him for money, so I thought, what harm can there be in that?

After a short time Frank came out with this guy and was just talking with him about traveling. They got in the back seat. I drove away from the bus station and about three blocks later I heard someone get hit. The guy jumps from the car, to the middle of the street, and this guy starts screaming, "HELP! HELP!" like a woman! Frank tells me to get the hell out of there and so I did.

On the way back to Troy, Frank shows me a wad of money and told me he had "rolled that gay dude." Boy, I knew then that I had to do something or my butt would be back in the can.

I figured the guy might have gotten my license plate number and might call the cops. If that was the case, they would be at my house waiting on me. As it turned out, the cops were not at my house when I arrived home.

About 9:00a.m. Monday morning, I was at my probation officers office. I told him what had happened over the weekend and who was involved. At the time, I didn't know that Frank was also on probation. I was not supposed to be around anyone who was on probation, nor was I suppose to be out after 11p.m.

To make a long story short, I ended up back in jail for another thirty days for violating my probation.

About five days before I got out of jail, I received divorce papers saying my wife wanted out of the marriage and I would never see my daughter again.

During my thirty day stay, my wife's parents came to Ohio and took my wife and my daughter back to Pennsylvania.

I was ok with the wife leaving but, I really didn't know how to deal with the fact that my daughter was gone. Thinking about it over the years, I realized she was not wrong in taking off because I seemed to be on a self- destructive path with my life at that time.

My mind is rolling along about three hundred miles an hour. I'm trying to put all the events that were going on at the time, in some sort of order so I don't bore my readers. But wait!! That is what this book is all about; you knowing me! Getting into serious trouble and then learning how to cope with the consequences that comes with it!

The Second Wife

Well, my thirty days were up and I was released from the city jail. I knew I had to find work, so I went back to work for Jim Mueller hanging and finishing drywall. I got so good at the trade that I was known as "the guy who could repair a damaged wall like it never happened."

My parents had this little shed behind their house and I asked if I could stay there for a while. Of course they said "sure." I dry walled, insulated, painted and fixed it up into a neat little place to live. I had a hot plate to cook on, a refrigerator and an old army cot to sleep on. I had a little car that my father helped me fix up. My life was once again, going in the right direction.

During one of my many stops at this little gas station in Potsdam, Ohio, I met this great looking young lady. Her name was Pat and I finally got her to go out with me after asking her what seemed a hundred times! We had a great time just being with each other.

I found out she was a reservations agent for Trans World Airlines. She had rented a place in the country near Potsdam, Ohio. She had enough ground to raise a horse she called Blaze.

Pat had two brothers, one older and one younger than her. They lived in Greenville, Ohio, where Pat went to school.

Now I found Pat to be a very nice woman and really thought I loved her. She was about 5' 9" tall and very good looking. She had blonde hair and a great figure! Pat used to model clothes on the Bob Braun television show.

I can't recall how long we dated, but we were married on July 23, 1965 just seven days after my divorce from my first wife was final.

We moved in together at her place and started a new life for ourselves. I told Pat about some of my previous problems and she agreed to work with me and help get our lives back on track.

She knew that I had a divorce court date coming up soon and we worked together to prepare for it.

The day the court hearing took place; my ex-wife did not even show up! She sent her attorney instead. It was the 16th of July 1965 when the divorce was granted and she got custody of my daughter and I was required to pay child support. I had no problem with paying child support. She is my daughter and I loved her very much. I was able to see her through my court ordered visitations for a short while.

Well, here's how that went. Every time I called to talk to my daughter, she was conveniently out of town, or at the doctor's office, or on vacation with her uncle. There was always a reason why I could not talk to her.

I contacted an attorney to see if I had any rights per the court order. The attorney told me that my ex- wife was in violation of the court order and I had every right to take her to court.

When I contacted the child support agency for help in locating my daughter, and asked them to enforce the court order, all I got was a bunch of run around. They just wanted to talk about the child support money that I was supposed to be paying. I hung up on them!

They did not know where she was or how to get in contact with her. They did not know if she had even been removed from the state of Ohio! She could have been out of the court's jurisdiction as far as I knew! After the child support agency told me they had no clue where my daughter was, I stopped making the child support payments. The court could not send her the money so I assumed they were just going to keep my money and give it to someone else and I was not happy with that. So Pat and I began looking for my daughter and found that my ex-wife had dumped my daughter Linda, off at her grandmothers and left!

My ex-mother-in-law was keeping Linda away from me because she just did not like me. This crazy woman believed that I was a "hit man" or a member of some underworld family! If I truly was, I think I would have had her whacked!

My wife was granted the divorce on July 16, 1965. For the next four or five years, the child support enforcement agency would drag me back to court demanding that I start paying my child support. They tried to also get poundage!

I always took my Attorney to court with me. He would ask the child support agency to tell us where Linda was. We ask where she went to school, who was her doctor, and was she, even alive! They simply could not or would not answer any of these questions. The court finally dismissed all charges

My wife Pat and I continued on with our lives. I was released from probation on March 13, 1968. Because I was still on probation when Pat and I married, we could not leave the state of Ohio. I had promised her a Disneyland honeymoon. As soon as I was off probation, Pat and I took off for California, to Disneyworld! We had a wonderful time! While in California, we visited with my Aunt Bessie and Uncle Earl. I wanted to show off my wife to them!

On our return home, we were actually able to make arrangements to go to Oreland, Pennsylvania to visit my daughter, Linda. The court had ordered Linda's grandmother to make her available to me for a visit. Pat and I drove her little blue Volkswagen bug out to Oreland, PA. to visit with my daughter.

THE ACCIDENT

We picked my daughter up after her grandmother read us the riot act. She told us that if we did not have her back in a couple of hours, she would call the police and have us arrested for kidnapping.

I guess she thought that I would take Linda and go back to Ohio! If I had known then what I know now, that's exactly what I would have done! They say hindsight is better than foresight when you don't know all the rules. So true!

The three of us headed out to find a place to eat and visit for a while. I was driving along when some guy crested a hill on my side of the road! I swerved to the right to keep from having a head on collision. I ran the car up on a small knoll causing the car to roll over.

I don't think the vehicle had seat belts, but none the less, all of us were thrown from the car. I landed on my side still hanging on to my daughter, Linda, for dear life. My wife Pat had landed on her back, on a pop bottle and slid across the road. Her back was severely cut. Linda was not injured and I had a broken finger but otherwise just skinned up.

I still recall Linda's grandmother yelling at me, saying, she knew this was going to happen because I was an irresponsible individual. She accused me of speeding or doing something stupid. That woman just could not believe that anyone else on earth could be dumber than me. I guess we all have an ax to grind.

Pat spent a week or so in the local hospital. After her release, Trans World Airlines agreed to fly us back home for free. I guess that was one of the perks that employees got, back then.

The first time that my past began to hound me was when we returned home from Pa... Our landlord, who was one of my class mates in school, and a busy body, found out, somehow, about my past criminal conviction. I have no idea who told my landlord about me, but she asks us to please vacate the house as soon as possible. What was she thinking? Did she think I was going to rob her? Another setback to deal with!

Pat's dad worked as a union carpenter out of the Dayton local union hall. She told me that he could help me get my journeyman's card and that way I could make good wages working as a carpenter. I went to the union hall and was initiated into local 2248 of Piqua, Ohio. I paid a one hundred thirty five dollar fee and received my local union membership book in October of 1967.

Then I got a job working for the B.G. Danis Construction Co. as a union journeyman millwright. Again, life was good. I had a great job and a lovely wife. What more could a man ask for?

While working on this job, I ran into some guys who

invited me to go to the local bar and have a drink or two with them. Just being social, I thought.

I started hanging out with these guys causing my home life to be disrupted. The wife wanted me home after work and most of the time I did go home. It was those times that I didn't go home that caused all the problems!

I became friends with people who worked in law-enforcement and they utilized me to get information on other criminal activities going on around the area. You were known as a snitch, or as some people called you, a confidential informant.

I was a pretty good informant if I say so myself! I continued working as a millwright and a confidential informant at the same time. The "job" is called a "cover." I became more knowledgeable in law-enforcement and was instrumental in helping solve some serious cases through Mr. Harlan Andrews from the Montgomery County Sheriff's Office.

Pat had a brother, who was a large guy. Before Pat and I married, I had had an encounter with him. At the time of the fight, I did not know he was Pat's brother.

I was in Greenville, Ohio with a couple of guys I worked with and we decided to stop and get something to eat at a Parkmour restaurant.

The guys in the car beside us invited us to the city park to have a rumble or what is commonly known as an "ass kicking contest."

We arrived at the city park. When I got out of my car I saw that this guy was much bigger than I was. I figured I'd go the "equalizer route." My equalizer was a tire iron and I chased him around the car a few times, running him off.

When Pat and I got married we actually recognized each other at the wedding reception that was held at her folk's house. He told me then, that he ran because he thought I was crazy. I guess I was a greater actor than Jack Nicholson in the movie "The Shining," although I wasn't crazy. I was just not going to allow a big guy to beat me up at that time or at any other time.

BAIT

THE BAIT SHOP

I met and befriended a police officer in Greenville Ohio, by the name of Roy Harrison. We got together and tried to start a bait shop. We both had invested quite a bit of money in it. We had bought water tanks, bait, fishing poles, and lures. Roy and I also invested in some scuba diving equipment, like tanks, regulators, wetsuits, depth gauges and such.

It was almost time to open the shop to the public. We cleaned the tanks, swept the floors and made the shop presentable. I noticed right away that when it came time to do some "work," it seemed like Roy's wife was never around and my wife was trapped at the bait shop every day. I was working construction and Roy was working his shift as a police officer. That left only the ladies to run the bait shop during the day.

When I got home from my job it was always me who had to close up each evening. After a short period of time, maybe six or eight weeks, Pat and I decided that we would close up the bait shop. We did not want to argue with Roy and his wife about their (nonexistent) part of running the bait shop. Ron and his wife were always there to collect their share of the profits at the end of each week! You could bet on that!

I took my part of the money that Pat and I invested, out in scuba diving equipment and whatever else I could recover. What I left was for Roy to do with as he pleased. I believe in the end, Pat and I took about a twelve hundred dollar loss on that little investment.

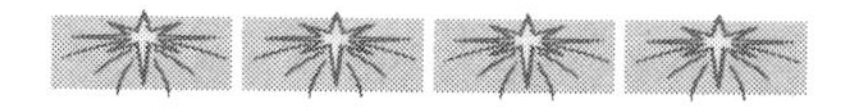

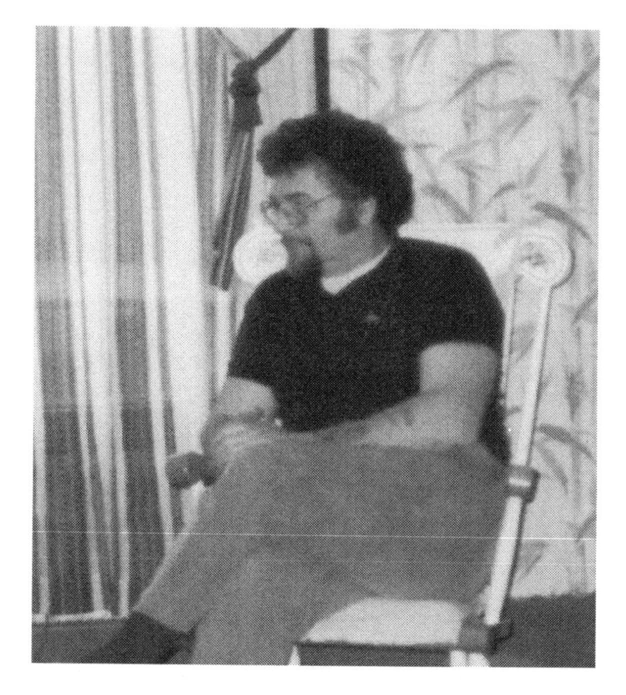

COVERT – OPS

These were some really confusing and tiring times. I tried to maintain my home life by working at the construction site but still get into the mainstream of the drug culture without becoming a part of it. I received a call from the Montgomery County prosecutor's investigator Harlan Andrews, (deceased) asking me to meet with him.

We met and he explained to me that I was working with a couple of fellows that his office felt was involved in a burglary ring in Montgomery County. Mr. Andrews gave me a couple of names I should try to hook up with.

So I proceeded to hang out with these guys and others that you run into at bars. We did a lot of drinking and other stuff that you normally do if you're a "rounder."

I guess you might say I was doing a covert operation. During this time I was having affairs with women, drinking, playing pool, getting into fights and other different things that I had to do while I was playing the part of a bar runner or rounder.

I was working on the Bell Telephone building in downtown Dayton with a guy by the name of Gordon. Gordon was on Mr. Andrews's list! I found out he was part of the burglary ring that was burglarizing homes and businesses in and around Montgomery County!

I went to his home one night and watched him and his friend Wayne, go through the items that they had stolen from a county commissioners home. I purchased some of the items: including a 9mm German Lugar hand gun. Later, I turned over this evidence to Harlan Andrews and told him, the guys put all the stuff they didn't want from the burglary in a sewer in downtown Dayton. I told Harlan that I was actually present when they were going through the goods!

I didn't know who it was that Gordon and his guys robbed at the time, but they had put all this stuff in pillowcases. Back at his home, they sorted out coin collections, guns, watches, and jewelry that they had taken while robbing this house.

They took what they didn’t want of the stolen goods, put it back in pillowcases, took it downtown Dayton and put in a city sewer line.

I distinctly remember that at the time there was a deputy sheriff involved in this burglary ring. The deputy was informing Gordon and his guys, who the people were that was going to be on vacation or out of town for whatever reason. These vacationers would ask the sheriff department to look over their house while they were gone. Hence, the deputy knew what homes Gordon and his guys could break into!

Somehow, after I gave all the information I had to Mr. Andrews, they were able to raid Gordon's place and arrested all of those that were involved. I did not have to reveal my identity nor did I have to testify in the trials about my involvement during the investigation. Boy was I ever glad about that!

I met a worker at the union hall whose name was Carl Brown. Carl told me he was from Silver City, New Mexico. I worked with him on numerous construction jobs in and around Dayton, including, BG Danis, Zigler, and Funderburg construction companies. Larry Funderburg and I were sitting in the union hall waiting for a "work call" from some company needing help.

A call came in requesting two "rough carpenters." Larry and I were sent to see a guy by the name of Leroy.

Payday at this job was weird. On Friday Leroy would give us our paychecks and have us endorse them! He would then give us the cash for them!

We thought this was a very unusual practice. We were going to say something to him about it, but we decided what the hell, it didn't matter as long as we got paid!

At the end of the year we did not get a W-2 from Leroy. We were sure glad we had kept our check stubs. They were the only proof of our income and how much taxes he had taken out.

We found out later that Leroy had taken the taxes out of our checks but had not paid a dime to the I.R.S... The last I heard of Leroy, he was on his way to prison for income tax evasion.

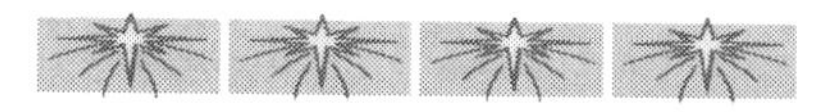

Pat and I bought a small ten acre mini farm just outside of New Madison, Ohio and lived there for a short time. She and I separated the first time because I was spending more time in the bars looking for criminals than what I should have been. I didn't want to tell her that I was working as an informant through the prosecutor's office. I thought it would jeopardize my marriage. I was too damn dumb to see my marriage was falling apart because "I didn't tell her!"

We separated again for the second time. I rented a sleeping room in Dayton, Ohio just a few blocks from where Gordon M. lived. My wife went back to live with her parents. I'm not exactly sure of the time frame in which this happened.

I ran across my buddy Carl Brown while looking for another construction job. Carl told me about a man in Greenville, Ohio who owned two semi tractors. Carl suggested we purchase the trucks and start a logging business.

Carl and I made an agreement with Mr. Fritz Martin to purchase his semi tractors. Mr. Martin was the owner of the local jewelry store in Greenville, Ohio.

One of the tractors was a cab over Mack and the other one was a GMC conventional gas rig. We also purchased two 32 foot trailers.

Carl and I used the trucks for our logging business that we had just started.

We would buy timber from a farmer, cut it down, and use a bulldozer to pull the logs from the wooded area. We loaded the logs on the trailers from the nearest lane or road to where we cut them. We hauled the logs to a saw mill in Hillsboro, Ohio. After a lot of wheeling and dealing for the best price we could get, we sold the logs to them. We would unload the timber and head back to get another load.

I was working steady as a union carpenter while I was still working in our logging business. If the carpenters union did not have a job for me to go to, I had the logging business to fall back on.

I was also going to Montgomery County, Ohio and building cases on information about stolen goods that I purchased from different thieves for the prosecutor's office.

At this time I was not a commissioned police officer. I was just working as a confidential informant and reported to the prosecutor's office. We met (out of town) somewhere on numerous occasions, so I could get paid for the information I was providing to them.

I was having "get togethers" on a regular basis with my wife Pat and we decided to try and work things out to save our marriage. We rented an apartment in Greenville, Ohio and started over again.

Things were going very good between my wife and me. I also was able to keep my undercover work tied into my regular job.

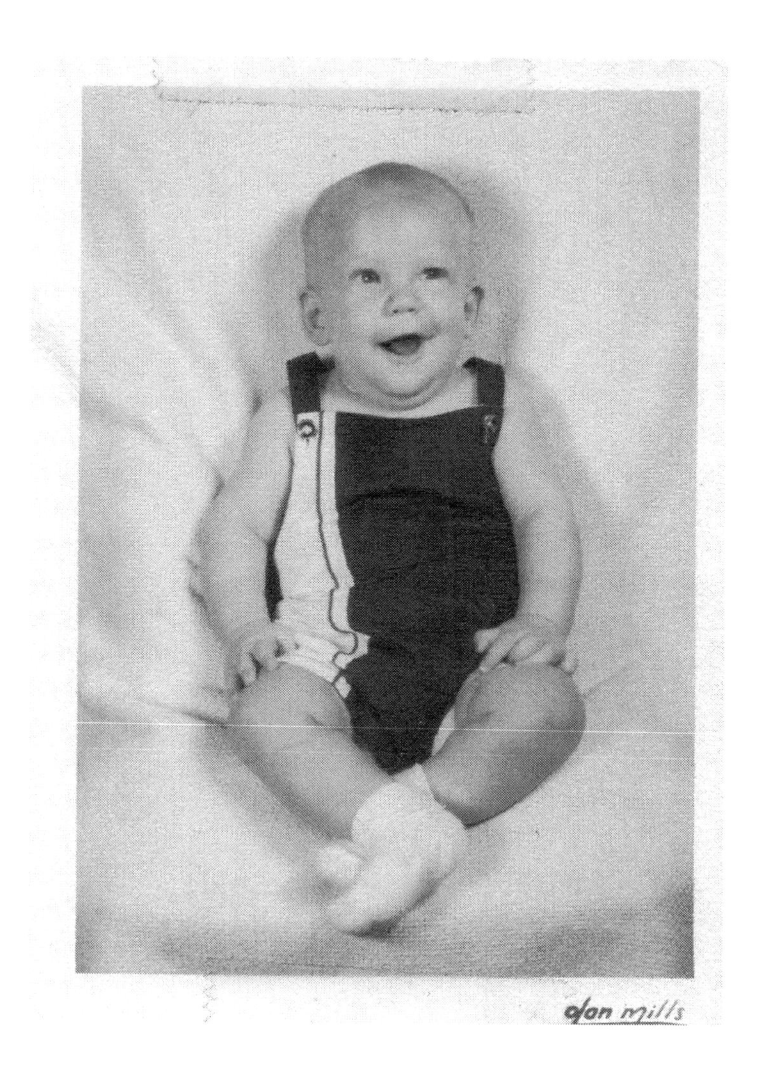
Olan Mills

OUR SON IS BORN

My wife informed me that she thought she was with child. We were so happy and started making preparations for our new addition to the family. Our son Gary David was born April 4, 1965 and what a blessing he was.

Shortly after David was born, I was working in our logging business when I received a serious head injury. I was unloading a trailer full of logs when a chain boomer broke. The load of logs fell from the trailer, pinning me between the trailer and this pile of fallen logs. My skull had been partially crushed.

I was in a coma for nine days. The doctors were telling my family that they didn't know if I would be ok or if I would be a vegetable the rest of my life. There are some people today, who say I have never been right since (jokingly of course)! Now we all know what's wrong with me!

Because I was unable to work, Pat went to work at a local restaurant called the Hasty Tasty. It was a place where all the kids hung out on Friday and Saturday nights.

It was at this time, I believe, that she met a guy named John Hopkins. I think she began having an affair with him.

While I was convalescing, I met some fellows who were trying to start a little country band. We would get together and practice playing music. Toni Stivers was the drummer. Howie Beam played lead guitar. Carl Brown played bass guitar and I tried to play rhythm. We were having some fun playing music at a bar in Ansonia, Ohio.

Our group was at the J.C. Hall practicing one evening and some of the guy's girlfriends came to hang around and watch. The girls were all standing in the back of the room when Pat came in. She looked around, and seeing the girls, she promptly got upset (assuming that one of them was there with me) and took off in a huff.

Again, Pat moved back into her parent's home taking our son with her. On April 6, 1968 I was served with papers asking for a divorce from the courts.

While we were separated I had run into a young lady who was a sister to one of the other girls there and we hit it off. We seemed to have a lot in common as far as liking the same music and just hanging around.

She was not a bad looking girl but in reality, I thought she was a Jesus freak. I was playing football with a bunch of local guys and she liked to come watch me play.

On January 10, 1969 Pat was awarded a divorce from me.

We used the same attorney because it was an uncontested divorce. We had made a full agreement on the terms and conditions set forth by the court.

I was paying my child support as ordered by the court and I thought everything was going well. I had gone to pick up David on a cold Friday night in early spring for my weekly visitation. I was informed by Pat's coworkers that she no longer worked at the bowling alley and no one knew where she had gone. One of the employees told me that Pat had told her she was leaving the state.

That was the last time I laid eyes on my son for many years. I believe he was sixteen years old before I saw him again.

By using contacts that I had in law enforcement and a never ending quest to find my son I continued looking for him. This was the same way I looked for my daughter Linda Lee. I will never figure out why Pat did not think I would find my son sooner or later.

For years I spent ungodly hours on the phone or the computer at the sheriff's office trying to find my daughter and son. I eventually found both of my children and I know where they are to this very day and have a great relationship with them both.

THE OFFICIAL RULES
ACCORDING TO
Gary

It's nearly impossible to put into a book everything that happened to me or around me during all this time. It would most likely be enough for two books maybe even more. During all this time, other things were going on in my life, like buying and selling homes, moving from one place to another because of a divorce or new job. I'm surprised I'm not an insane man by now!

I worked on a job where I saw Gordon M. fall fifteen feet off a wall and land on his head! He got up, shook it off and went back to work like nothing happened! I've seen other guys fall off walls and equipment, and was hurt really bad or killed.

I got into it with supervisors, messed around other workers equipment, nailed working helmets to work benches and played jokes on lots of people. We never committed any serious violation of the law. I'm sure OSHA wouldn't agree with that statement!

One time Larry Funderburg and I was working on the sixth floor of the new Bell Telephone building in downtown Dayton. We observed this laborer letting down a large 8 x 8 piece of lumber over the side of the building. This piece of lumber looked like a super giant railroad tie. He was trying to lower it to the ground, six stories below.

He was letting it down one end at a time as if to keep it from getting away from him.

Larry and I went over to where this guy was working and ask him, "What is going to stop that piece of lumber from falling and killing someone if it gets away from you?" He simply shrugged his shoulders and said, "I don't know."

Jokingly, I thought I would help him out. I told him that he had to loop the rope around his ankle so that if that thing got away from him and started falling he could stand still, acting like an anchor!

It was shortly thereafter that the supervisor came up to that floor and about crapped when he saw the guy lowering these large timbers down to the ground with it looped around his leg! I guess he ask the guy, what the hell he was doing with his foot wrapped up with that rope. The guy said that Larry and I had told him that it was the safest way to lower the timber without hurting anyone. Boy did Larry and I catch hell for that little escapade!

I remember being assigned to "hanging all the doors" in the building. The doors were delivered to the ground floor and Carl and I had to pull the doors up the elevator shaft to whatever floor we were working on. They were big steel doors that weighed about thirty five pounds each. I remember hanging every single door in that building, mainly by myself because Carl had been transferred to another job location.

It took me pretty close to nine months to hang all the doors and install all the hardware on them. When I finished with that job, I remember just walking up the alley to the next job.

The building was going to be a Holiday Inn Motel. I worked on that building for some time. I did not like Ralph, the supervisor. I got into it with him because he wanted me to tear the plywood forms off of the inside of the elevator shaft. It couldn't be done because they were stuck in place. Someone had failed to spray the proper amount of oil on the forms.

As I tried to get the plywood loose, Ralph began yelling at me to get a large crowbar to get it loose. He said the crane was waiting on me.

I told Ralph that if I used a crowbar it would punch a hole in it, rendering it useless.

Ralph ordered me to get that plywood off the wall, so I took a four foot crowbar and tried to pry it off. Guess what! It punched a hole in it, just like I said it would!

Ralph came unglued and called me a son of a bitch! I told him not to be calling me names and not to be bringing my mother into this and if he said anything like that again I was going to kick his butt. He didn't listen and called me a son of a bitch again! I punched him and he fell down the elevator shaft, which at that time was only a fifteen foot drop. In the bottom of the elevator shaft was about six to seven feet of cold water! He didn't really get hurt, but he did get wet and cold. Talk about sweet revenge!

I went down to the supervisor's office and told them that I wanted my check; because I had just knocked Ralph into the elevator shaft and he would most likely fire me anyway.

Bob, who was the job superintendent, ask Ralph and I both what had happened. We told our sides of what happened. Bob told me to go back to doing my job and Ralph must have been fired because I never saw him after that.

When we finished that job, the union hall sent me to work for Funderburg Construction Company in Dayton. We were building officers' quarters at Wright Patterson Air Force Base.

Some of the guys wore sleeveless t-shirts during the summer months and some wore shirts that had been ripped off to the belly button, to stay cool. There were lady officers on the base and they complained that the guys working out there were half naked in shorts and cutoff shirts. The base commander came down to the job site and told everybody we had to wear, at a minimum, a full length T-shirt with a pocket on it. So a bunch of us cut the sleeves off of our t- shirts and sewed a pocket on them. We did cover up our midriffs but still continued to wear our shorts.

We were just trying to stay cool while getting our job done, even if it meant bending the rules to get it accomplished.

Talk about bending the rules! The ironworkers got all ticked off at Larry and me for supposedly doing their job! They said that Larry and I were trying to put up junior beams that were made out of steel and it was considered an ironworkers job.

The problem was, at this time, the ironworkers were out on strike! When the ironworkers found out what we were doing, they went to the union office and filed grievances to stop us from doing "their" jobs.

The ironworker's union representative came to the job and informed Larry and I not to touch their welding equipment or anything else belonging to the welding crew.

We finished that job and went to work on a new Kroger store that was being built in Fairborn, Ohio. After just a few days on this job, a union representative came to the job site and tried to collect what they call "check off dues" from the guys on the job who owed this. This money amounted to two cents an hour for every hour we worked.

This representative became very heated about collecting fifty six cents from me. He said I owed for twenty eight past hours. I told him I didn't have fifty six cents, and he would have to come back Friday and I would give it to him. He said he was going to throw me off the job if I did not pay him the money. I told him that if he attempted that, I would throw him off the damn cooler. The representative swelled up and said to me “give me the money or else.” So I tossed him off the top of the walk-in freezer that we were working on at the time.

The union representative came back the following Friday, and I paid him the money. I told him that he could have saved himself a lot of time and bruises if he had just came back this Friday in the first place.

That's just how those union representatives were in those days.

FIRE AT THE BAR

I continued working for different construction companies while continuing my work with the local prosecutors' offices.

I was in Montgomery County, working a covert operation at a bar on North Dixie Highway, called Angie's tavern. I was just sitting around with probably thirty or forty people having a drink and talking with my friend Harold. Harold was one of my coworkers on construction jobs around the Dayton area. Harold did not know I worked the bars at night looking for illegal activities.

We (Harold and I) were sitting in Angie's tavern talking about this and that. A waitress by the name of Faye (who was quite the looker) was waiting on us. Angie's bar was a gathering place for some of the guys that I was working with and also a lot of Dayton's bad asses. All the while, I was trying to gather information on burglaries and other crimes that I hoped to hear about. We were sitting at a table in the back of the bar where it was smoky (I do not smoke) and people were talking and yelling. Harold Goff had gone up to the bar to order another drink and ended up in an arguing match with a big dude. They decided, after arguing for a bit, they were going to go outside and duke it out.

They were probably arguing over some slut. Who knows!

Harold, being a tall man and in good physical condition, proceeded to punch this big bear of a man out as he circled him. This guy was so big that if he had gotten hold of Harold, he probably would have crushed him. Herald just danced around and kept punching him in the face and body like he was pro boxer.

Pretty soon somebody came running out and started yelling "the police are coming!" By the time the police got there, everybody was back inside the bar just talking and carrying on like nothing had happened. The big dude must have gotten in his car and left because I didn't ever see him after that.

Everyone had been back in the bar for about an hour or so, when I noticed a lot of smoke just kind of rolling up against the ceiling. Nobody else seemed to notice this going on! Not wanting to cause a panic, I called Fay over to where I was sitting. I told her the building was on fire and she should ask everyone to leave.

She looked at me bluntly and said, "Your crazy and quit pulling my leg!" I told her again, "Fay, I'm telling you, the damn building is on fire and we need to get everyone out of the place!"

I got up to go outside when she looked at the ceiling and seen all this smoke.

By this time, the smoke was gathering quite badly and going from a lighter gray to a darker black color.

Fay started to scream, "The bar's on fire! The bar's on fire!" Everybody was trampling over each other to get the hell out of the place.

The fire department arrived and had the fire under control in a short time, but there was a lot of water damage. The fire had burned about half the roof off. The water damage made a big mess of everything in the place. It seemed like it took six or seven months to rebuild it. Angie's tavern did eventually open back up.

We found out later that someone had crawled up into the attic through the access panel in the men's restroom, dumped some oil or kerosene, and tossed a match on it. To this day, I don't think they ever did figure out who the person was that started the fire.

I knew of a guy who was a known "firebug." Herbie hung out at Angie's all the time. I always thought it was him that started the fire but could not remember seeing him in the bar that night. I do recall another night when someone gave Herbie fifty cents and a bottle of beer to burn a guy's car that was sitting across the street!

Now keep in mind, this car was a 1959 Ford retractable hardtop! Herbie didn't care what kind of car it was. He only wanted to burn something. Maybe fifteen minutes later, everybody in Angie's tavern began yelling that there was a car on fire!

That once beautiful 1959 Ford was just absolutely engulfed in flames from bumper to bumper! By the time the fire department got there, the car was absolutely destroyed.

I can still remember seeing Herbie standing on the corner, rubbing his hands together and getting off on seeing those flames.

Later on, my girlfriend, her cousin Selda and I were at another bar in Dayton called the Glass Crutch, when I saw Herbie next. We were sitting around the table having a drink when Herbie pulled out a gun. He started waving the gun around, threatening to shoot me. I knew he was drunk and just being stupid. I told him to put that thing away before I took it away from him and shove it up his butt! Herbie put away the firearm, got up from his chair and left. I can't remember ever seeing Herbie after that.

At the end of that investigation, there were four or five guys arrested. After a search warrant was obtained, police recovered firearms, hand grenades, and other assorted stolen goods from a house on Gettysburg Ave.

Just like the last "take down" it involved some police officers. They were setting up the burglaries to homes whose owners were on vacation.

THIRD AND FINAL MARRIAGE

I actually dated and married one of the girls that was at the band practice that Pat had gotten so upset about. I started dating her after Pat left me. We were still seeing each other when Pat and I's divorce was finalized.

I had been in Dayton with her brother Larry, just messing around. After a fun evening, Larry dropped me off at my car, which I had parked on the street in Greenville, Ohio. I noticed someone sleeping in my car! Barb told me that her dad threw her out of the house because he found out that she was dating a married man! I took Barb to my apartment in Laura, Ohio. I had to explain to my landlord that we had gotten married because his faith would not have permitted him to allow us to live together, unmarried!

My landlady decided to have a wedding reception for us. She invited some of her church members. We received cookware, a toaster, dishes, glasses, silverware and other items to help us start a home. Little did she know that we were not married at the time.

My present father- in- law took care of that by telling them for us. They ask us to vacate the property. Barb's dad just did not like his daughter living with me and not be married.

I had moved to a small house trailer on Daleview Ave in Dayton, Ohio and Barbara moved back home to her parents place. Her brother Larry, who was A.W.O.L. from the Marine Corp, moved in with me for a short time. Larry and I went out on the town many times and once in awhile would bring ladies home with us for the night.

One morning Larry came into my room asking me if I had got a good look at the girl I had brought home. I answered "no" and after looking at her, I told her to "get out!" Larry did the same thing to the girl that was with him. They had followed us home in their own car, and when we told them to "get out" they jumped in the car and left! Larry and I have had many laughs over the years whenever this story comes up.

During all this time, my girlfriend Barb was coming to the house on the weekends and cleaning the place up for me.

There were times when she came over that I had to put her picture back on the wall because I had taken it down when I had other women over. (MY BAD?)

One weekend she came to clean the trailer and advised me she was going to have my baby!!!! WHAT!!! She ask me if I was going to marry her. Of course I told her I would and we proceeded to make preparations for an upcoming wedding and baby.

Barb's brother Scott had a Triumph motorcycle for sale so we went to Greenville, Ohio to buy the bike. On the way back home it began to rain. Barb was following me in our old Ford Falcon station wagon, the only car we owned at the time.

It started raining really hard and I was getting soaking wet. I was only riding about forty miles per hour when a guy came up behind me blowing his horn and waving at me. I pulled over to the side of the road to see what this guy wanted. He told me that my "wife" had wrecked the car on a curve behind me.

I turned around and hauled ass back to where the guy said she had left the road. Upon arrival, I found her still sitting in the car. The car looked like it had rolled over at least once and my carpentry tools had been strewn all over a muddy cornfield. The back door of the station wagon had been torn off and the glass broken and scattered all over the place.

The most important thing of all for me to do was to see how Barb and the baby were. She was about six months along with our baby, so yes I was worried about both of them!

I asked her if she was hurt and all she kept asking about was those damn tools that were scattered all over the muddy cornfield. I made sure Barb was ok and took off on the bike to West Milton, Ohio which was only about six miles up the road.

I got my father, who worked at the Sohio gas station, to bring the wrecker to pull the car from the ditch.

What really scared the crap out of me was when we pulled the car out of the ditch. There was the fuel tank, full of gas, laying in the muck where it had been broken off from the car! To this day, I am so thankful that she did not smoke while she was pregnant. If she had lit up a cigarette, it is highly possible that she and the baby would not be here today.

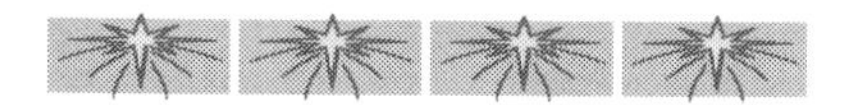

We set the wedding date for May 24th, 1969. My final divorce hearing from Pat was January 10th of the same year.

Barbara continued living with her parents until the wedding day. I was still working in construction and as an informant for Montgomery County.

On or about the first of May, I decided to go to Texas with my friend Carl. He wanted to do some elk hunting in the hills of Texas and I thought it would be neat to see things you only got to see in pictures. Seeing things in person would show the true beauty of Gods creations.

I kept calling Barb and telling her that I would be back to marry her on the 24th of May and not to worry.

Barb told me that her mother did not think I would come back from Texas, to marry her. She said that she would believe it when she heard me say "I do" and not until then. Barb's dad kept telling her I would not show up for the wedding, right up to the day of the wedding (Oh ye of little faith!)!

On May 24, 1969, I showed up at the church about ten minutes before the wedding was supposed to start. We were married on the upswing of the clock between 7:30 and 8:00 p.m. at the Meadowview Baptist Church in Laura, Ohio. I firmly believe that the myth of being married on the upswing of the clock means your marriage will always grow from there. I remember well when the pastor asked me to repeat the wedding vows; I turned to Barb's mother and said loudly, "I DO."

After the wedding, I moved Barb into my tiny trailer on Daleview Ave in Dayton. The little house trailer was just that, tiny. It only had one bedroom, a small kitchen and living room combination and a glass enclosed porch. It may have been small but it was comfortable. Barb's brother Larry had already moved out to a better hiding place because he was still AWOL from the Marines.

Our daughter Misty was born August 25 of that year. We started making a home for ourselves and our new baby. We placed a bassinet beside the bed next to Barb so that she could tend to Misty when it became necessary.

It was time to get back into the work force. Mr. Andrews had given me some information about a gambling game moving around the county. He gave me a couple names of the suspected players and asks me to see if I could get any information on this activity.

One of the names that I received was the owner of a service station on north Dixie Highway called Vince's Sunoco. I began frequenting his place of business by getting my oil changed, getting fuel, and generally hanging around.

While getting to know Vince and some of the other people that just came and went, I kept over hearing Vince talking about card games. He said he loved to play poker but his wife was giving him grief over wasting the business' money on gambling.

This little scam only lasted three or four weeks and did not amount to anything more than a few guys playing for nickels and dimes.

I had been to Angie's tavern, just sitting around and listening to conversations. The normal group was not there, so I got on the bike and headed home. I got about three blocks down the road when the local police tried to pull me over for some unknown reason. I couldn't think of any laws I had broken to give him reason to pull me over. Stupid me took off like a bat out of hell riding around the traffic circle about three times, leaving the police car behind in the dust, so to speak. I arrived at my house trailer, parked the bike behind the house and covered it up with a tarp. I went inside and went to bed.

I was working for Funderburg Construction Company in Dayton, Ohio whose owner was Leonard Funderburg. One of his sons worked for the company and he and I became very good friends. Larry and I spent many nights in the bars around Dayton, including our favorite: Angie's Tavern, just looking for women, drinking and fun. Of course Larry did not know, but I always had my eyes and ears peeled for illegal activities!

On one occasion we picked up two gals and went to an old railroad overpass located just off Stanley Avenue. Larry and I did the old coin toss. He lost, so I grabbed a blanket from the car, went down under the trestle and proceeded to get laid.

The lady and I had gotten bit all over our bodies by those blood sucking mosquitoes! Now came the hardest part, trying to explain away that many bites to the wife! Thanks to my quick thinking, I told her that I had to take a dump out in "mother nature," and before I could get finished, I had gotten eaten alive by those damn mosquitoes!

This time period also reminds me of the close encounter Larry and I had with his new automobile. It was a brand new Pontiac convertible, called "The

Judge." The Judge had a four speed standard transmission with a 389 cubic inch tri power engine.

As the story goes, Larry and I were on our way home from work when Larry decided to pass this slow moving "Sunday driver" going about forty five miles an hour. He down shifted the car and floored it to get around this guy. When the tires broke loose, the car went into a spin! After spinning around a couple of times, the car left the road going in reverse! We went over the embankment and headed down towards the dam! Larry got the car stopped about fifteen or twenty feet from the water's edge at the Huffman Dam!

I also remember the foreman on this job that Larry and I were working on. His name was Fred Lens. For some reason or other, Fred did not like me that well and was always trying to find some reason to fire me.

One day I had ridden my motorcycle to work and at the end of the day, I agreed to meet Larry at a night club called The Living Room. On our way to the night club we came up behind Fred, in his Chevy corvair, driving about five miles an hour under the speed limit. Larry tore around him in his GTO, "The Judge!" I decided to give Fred a "thrill of his life!' I stood up on the seat of the bike, and passed him going about seventy miles an hour! Fred hated me even more after that incident! He said I was a crazy man! Maybe so!

Fred never could understand how Larry and I could

work so much faster than the other guys. He figured we were doing something wrong or leaving something undone. He went to the owner of the company and told him he wanted me off the job.

Now mind you, I was working with the owners' son, Larry! We were not doing anything but busting our butts to get the job done. After the owner spoke with Larry and me, and saw that we were doing everything according to blueprint, he fired Fred! Mr. Funderburg told him to pick up his check at the office and told Larry and I to go on back to work!

Larry and I worked and ran around together for quite some time, and he still doesn't know to this day that I was also working covert operations at the same time. My bosses and I have laughed about this many times over the years.

HUMMM JOB

I can't seem to remember which year the motorcycle endorsement law went into effect but I believe it was around 1968 or 1969. Anyway, I was on my way to the house one afternoon when I spotted a deputy following me. I was careful to make sure my driving was in accordance with the moving traffic rules since I did not have my motorcycle endorsement yet.

I came to a stop sign about four blocks from the house. I made sure that I had made a complete stop, and turned right towards my home. The deputy turned his "overheads" on and stopped me for whatever! He came up to the bike and asks me for my driver's license and registration. I gave him both of these items without any fuss at all because I knew I was going to get cited for not having a motorcycle endorsement. What I did not know was that he was giving me a hum job, you know, (hum, I think I will just give this guy a ticket for the hell of it) just to be doing it.

He took my paperwork and asks me to accompany him to his patrol car. I complied and got in the front passenger seat and was waiting for him to give me the citation.

He got on his radio, talked for a few minutes and then asks that a wrecker be sent. I began thinking he was going to tow my bike to an impound lot!

My house trailer was only about fifty yards from my view, so I got out of the deputy's car and proceeded to push the bike to my house. The deputy came up behind me, jerked me away from the bike allowing it to fall to the ground. Now I was really pissed! He grabbed me again and tried to handcuff me.

By this time I was pretty "steamed." I told him, "If you want me to go downtown with you, it's not necessary for you to handcuff or manhandle me." That statement did not go over too well. He grabbed me again, turned me around, and tried to cuff me again! He pushed me, face forward, over this large rock that was in some guy's front lawn.

I somehow got my leg up high enough to push him back off of me. He fell on his butt in their front yard. He just didn't know when to stop! He jumped up and approached me again. I told him again that he was not going to cuff me and that if he wanted to go downtown I would be more than glad to go with him.

By this time a crowd of people had gathered. When he grabbed me for the third time, I grabbed him and threw him on the ground. I had his head between my legs and proceeded to jerk his shirt out and took the cuffs from him. I let him up and told him if he touched or grabbed me again, I was going to knock his teeth out.

During this time, the wrecker guy ran to the deputy's patrol car and called for backup. I began hearing sirens and knew that help was on the way. I put the handcuffs on myself, got in the patrol car and closed the door.

It wasn't long until more police officers showed up. By then, everything was under control except for Officer Mass getting his composure back together. I had ruffled his feathers pretty badly!

When the other officers arrived, I remember this highway patrolman coming over to the deputy's car. He opened the door, pointed his gloved finger in my face and said, "It's a good thing you are in that car punk." I replied, "It sure is or I would be out there kicking your butt too!"

I was taken to the Montgomery County Justice Center and put in a holding cell. I was ordered to back up to the cell door and they took the cuffs off. I guessed they were typing up multiple violations on me!

To my surprise, other officers that were there, came over to the cell and told me they wanted to shake my hand! WHAT? They said I had done them a big favor in bringing Officer Mass to the reality that the badge only covered a small portion of his body!

I was allowed to make a phone call to my lawyer which at the time was the prosecutor. It wasn't but a short time later a deputy came to me saying, "I don't know who you are or who you know but you are out of here!" I was on my way home!

About three weeks later I went to Vandalia Municipal Court with my attorney and the whole citation was tossed out of court. Imagine that!

It was shortly after the "humm job" incident that the county handed down multiple indictments for various crimes and warrants for the people involved.

Then it came time for the prosecutor's investigator to introduce the undercover guy (me) to the deputies and police officers who were going to serve these papers, and arrest the people involved.

To see the face of Deputy Mass and the other officers who helped him with the "humm job," was priceless!

We actually became friends after that and laughed about that episode many times.

MOVING AGAIN

Barb and I moved to Ginghamsburg, Ohio later in 1969 and actually lived in our first real house, instead of an apartment or tiny house trailer.

It was on a Sunday evening, Larry and I had shut down the card game and was cleaning up the place. We both had been drinking some. I finished off a partial bottle of Jim Beam and I ask Larry if we had anything else to drink. He produced a bottle of Cold Duck wine and he and I finished it off.

Well, needless to say, I was not in the proper shape to drive around the block let alone thirteen or fourteen miles back to Ginghamsburg. I did it anyways and arrived home safely. I remember crawling across the lawn to the front door. I was quietly trying to get into the house without waking Barb and the baby.

I did alright until I tried to get into the bed. I became so sick it was unreal. I figured if I could hurl and get all of that liquor out of me, it would help me to get over it faster. I remember hanging my head over the "throne," and my legs going numb! I kicked the bathroom wall and boy did I catch it from Barb!

The next morning when I got up to go to work, I asked Barb if she was going to fix me something to eat. She promptly replied, "Fix it yourself!" I then told her, "No food! No work!" and went back to bed.

I felt so bad that day, that I swore to myself I would never do that again! I can remember only one other time that I came close to getting that drunk!

Now Ginghamsburg was only about three miles from Tipp City, Ohio. The Chief of police of this city was Jack Cheadle at the time. Remember earlier when I was on probation? Well, Jack was my probation officer for the five years I was on probation. I got to know him very well. Jack was the guy who set me up with different police departments, to work covert operations.

Just mentioning Jack, reminds me of an incident that happened on my way back to the house one afternoon. I approached the street from the parking lot, looked to my left and saw a car approaching with his right turn signal flashing. I assumed he was going to turn into the parking lot. I started to pull out and nearly got broad sided by this person! I guess he had failed to turn off his turn signal from an earlier turn.

We did not collide, so we both proceeded to the intersection of St. Rt. 571 and Dixie Highway. We both stopped for the traffic signal. The guy proceeded to call me a stupid driver and using some very vulgar language. That upset me somewhat because he "involved my mother." He said something about kicking my butt and I told him that the only thing between him and I, was his car! He got out of his car; I got out of mine and was waiting on him.

When he came around the corner of his car I decked him! When he fell back onto the bumper of his car, I gave him a swift kick for the statement about my mom and drove off leaving him in the street.

About an hour or so later I received a call from the chief of police in Tipp City. Jack said he would like for me to come into his office for a chat.

I drove to town as requested. Upon arrival, I observed the gentleman that I had the encounter with sitting in the outer office of the police station. I knew then that this guy had run to the police and cried like a baby.

Chief Cheadle asks me to tell him my side of the story in regards to the incident. I told Jack the complete details of what happened. He asked me if I had kicked the guy after he was down. I replied, "That just did not happen. His injury was gotten when he had fallen on the bumper of his car."

Jack called the other guy into his office. He told the guy that he should feel "lucky" because if he had called his mother the same name, it would have been much worse than it was. Jack told this guy that he knew me well and he thought the guy got off easy. Jack told us both that we need to be more cautious and courteous when driving.

I left Jack's office, went back home and continued to try and live a normal life.

Heap-Ah

RED NECK RACE CAR

While living in Ginghamsburg, I decided to build a race car for the drag strip. I started gathering an engine, chassis, axles, and all other pieces to assemble something resembling a '23 ford t-bucket.

Now when Jeff Foxworthy talks about rednecks, I guess I fall into that group! I put together a small block 283 cubic inch engine in the living room floor. I had it hanging from a homemade engine stand and boy did the wife like that. Ha-ha!

The engine was close to being finished, but still needed the heads and the intake manifold put on. It was not as heavy as a finished engine so I decided to go ahead and place it in the car.

My brother-in- law and I carried it out to the awaiting chassis by hand. A short time later I had it up and running

I decided to take it for a test drive up old Route 25 toward Tipp City. Yes, I knew it was not legal to drive on the highway, but thought what the hell. I wasn't going to go too far and the police would not see me anyways.

I got away with that little trick two or three times till one of the neighbors called the highway patrol. A Highway Patrolman showed up at the house and asks me if I had been on the road with that race car. I said,

"Only to back it up to turn it around." He advised me that it was illegal and if he caught me on the road, he would ticket me. I agreed not to have the car on the road as long as it was illegal. I did exactly as I promised. I put tags on the car and made sure it was street legal before I drove it on the road again.

I towed that redneck car to a drag strip just outside of Piqua, Ohio and had a good time racing it. I never made any money at the races but I sure surprised a lot of people as to how fast that thing would go!

I took the car to Kilkare Drag Strip. The crazy car was hard to control and I ended up knocking down the "christmas lights" and ran into a fence. I finally sold that redneck of a race car and later got a different car to work on.

We moved to this large farm house that was on a chicken farm. The house came with the job. The job: managing a poultry farm with thirty thousand chickens! Eggs were gathered, checked, sized, packaged and sold to many different stores and markets. Of course we had eggs galore at our disposal!

I took care of and made all the repairs to the farm equipment. I managed ten employees starting our work day at 4a.m. seven days week. Barb and I took turns on the weekends and my brother-in-law Jim helped out a lot.

I was still making cases on people who were stealing goods and selling drugs around the area for any agency that wanted to pay me for doing so.

My wife and I took care of the chicken farm for a little over a year when I got a job working maintenance at the Darke County Home in Greenville, Ohio. I worked for the Darke County Home about a year then on to the next job at the Service Beauty Supply Company in Greenville. We moved from the chicken farm to West Third Street in Greenville which was much closer to my job.

I worked in the warehouse at Service Beauty Supply, filling sales orders.

While working the warehouse one day, I ran into a guy who was a security guard for the Wackenhut Security Company.

He told me they were looking for security guards for the staff at Sheller Globe Manufacturing in Union City, Indiana. He said he would put in a good word for me if I would put in an application. So I did.

Now is when things began coming back to haunt me of the bad times that I had gotten into a few years back.

I filled out the application and just did not fill in anything that had to do with my past. To my amazement, I was hired!

I quit the Service Beauty Supply Company and became a full time Wackenhut Security Guard.

They issued me a uniform and badge. I was trained on how to "hit the keys" while making my rounds through the plant. I found it very enjoyable and loved every minute of this job.

The guys name that put in a good word for me, was Nick Abling. Nick was also a police officer for the Union City, Ind. police department. Nick and I became good friends and I road with him on a few occasions while he was on patrol. A lot of the town people thought that I was a police officer when Nick would make a traffic stop.

Nick was a very short fellow and stood about five foot five inches or so and weighed, maybe, one hundred sixty pounds soaking wet. He was very broad shouldered and quite pumped for such a small guy. Not one time did I ever see Nick back down from anybody. It didn't matter how big they were or how bad they seemed to be.

One evening, I remember it very well; Nick brought this fellow in for being publicly intoxicated. The guy tore Nick's shirt trying to get to his badge. In an instant, Nick had this guy bent over the desk backwards. I would swear to this day, he had his shoes hooked onto this guy's belt and was slapping him upside his head with his slapjack!

I was sworn in as a part time police officer shortly thereafter in this same little town, Union City. Again, to my amazement, I figured my past would come up but it never did during my tenure there.

I started working the streets as a sworn patrol officer for the first time in my life. I still wonder if the department actually ran a record check on my background. I assumed they had not.

Whenever the Chief ask me to work and I was available, I did so as soon as I got off from working security at the plant.

During this span of time, Barb and I had purchased a new home in Wayne Lakes, Ohio.

FIRST FULL TIME POLICE JOB

Barb and I were still residing at Wayne Lakes when I applied for a position as a police officer in the village of Versailles, Ohio. Much to my amazement, I was hired on as a full time Versailles Police Officer.

One of the requirements of being a police officer in this small village was; you had to live inside the village limits. My brother-in-law, Rick Riffel, owned a semi tractor trailer. About a week before Christmas of 1975, he came to the house and we loaded most of everything we owned into that trailer. The last item to be loaded in the trailer was an already decorated Christmas tree. I don't know how we made the trip safely but we did. It was a snowy dark night, the roads were covered with ice and visibility was poor at best.

I got along just great with almost every person I met in this village. I was having a great time utilizing my past experience on both sides of the law.

I knew what it was like to be arrested, handcuffed and taken to jail. I remembered how I was treated or mistreated by some of the officers involved. I truly understood how to treat other people no matter how bad they seemed to be.

An event comes to mind. Things were going pretty slow on the streets, until I received a weird call from a lady. She called in telling the chief that someone was disturbing her flower pots and making a lot of racket in her back yard. The chief told me this lady had made this same complaint on numerous occasions and he knew she was an elderly person who seemed to hear things and imagine others.

I told him I would try to appease the lady and he told me to do whatever it took, short of shooting her. I went to the lady's home, and after knocking, she answered the door. She proceeded to show me some very beautiful flowers on her porch. You could tell that they had been well cared for. I listened as she was telling me that someone had "moved" them on her porch. They would "move" her flowers from one spot to another and mess around in her back yard.

It was just after dark. I told her I would check out her back yard and see what I could find.

I went behind her home and after a few minutes I took my service revolver and fired it into the ground in a safe area as to not endanger anyone. I came back to her porch, told her that I had taken care of her problem and I did not feel she would be bothered again by those noises.

She thanked me and I continued on with my duties. As far as I know, the lady never did call in a complaint of any kind after that.

There were numerous incidents that happened during my time on this police department and some just stand out more than others.

A couple of instances come to mind right away and the first came on a warm evening about one hour after sundown. We received a complaint about a neighbor yelling, being drunk and disturbing everyone within hearing distance. Officer Tom Cool and I answered the call. When we arrived at the scene, we observed a guy (known to us as John Subler.) go into the house. Tom went up on the porch and requested John to come outside so we could talk to him. When John came out onto the porch, his hair looked as if he just came out of the shower and was obviously under the influence of alcohol or some other substance. He produced a small caliber rifle and instantly pushed it into Tom's belly threatening to shoot him if he did not get off his property.

I was standing on the steps and thought to myself; this could turn real ugly really quick and I instantly took Johns legs out from under him by a swift swing of my night stick. I hit his legs just below the knees and on the front of his shin bones.

When he came down, he landed with his face on the breach of the firearm, splitting his lips and making his nose bleed very badly. After the ambulance took him to the hospital, he was patched up then taken to the county lockup. I believe he was charged with aggravated assault and went to jail for six months or so. I'm not really sure because I was not with the department when he received his sentencing.

The biggest event that went down during my tenor in Versailles was on a Saturday morning about 2 a.m. on October 21, 1975.

I tried to arrest a young man for public intoxication. He was walking with a young lady and was just being a butthole by giving me the finger as I drove by. I guess he was trying to show off for the girl. I stopped the patrol car, got out and ask if he was ok or if he had a problem of some sort. He started yelling and pushing me.

I advised Mr. Litton that he was under arrest for assaulting me and he took off running. I chased him for about a block and struck him in the back of the head with my night stick, fracturing his skull in the process.

After I had him in custody I called for the ambulance to take him to the hospital. He was bleeding somewhat and I was concerned I may have hit him too hard.

While waiting for the squad to show up, four or five other people came and tried to take Bobby away from me. The group was threatening me and one person actually hit me in the face, breaking my glasses. I drew my weapon and ordered all of them to stand back. They all got in their automobiles and blocked my patrol car to keep me from leaving.

I placed a call to the Darke county sheriff's office for assistance, and upon their arrival, (about the same time the life squad arrived,) all the bad guys took off and tried to hide.

All the people were found hiding under cars, in the bushes and other places. Every one of them were arrested, taken to the county jail and later charged with various violations including assaulting a police officer.

In retaliation of this event, the following Wednesday, the Chief of police (who owned the Shady Rest Service Station) closed the place of business and stopped at the Valley View Inn for a beer on the way home. The chief was attacked by three people who were involved in the Saturday arrest of Mr. Litton.

Chief Frantz was taken to the Wayne Hospital in Greenville with a broken leg, possible skull fracture, eye injury and multiple bruises and small cuts.

Every one of the people involved in beating up the Chief, went to prison or county jail for a period of time for their part in the beating.

THE BLOODY CADILLAC

In the summer of 1973, on a Saturday night, my next door neighbor Dan and his wife Patty, and my wife and I decided to go to a dance in Versailles, Ohio at a place called the Crystal Ball.

It was the disco era and I wore a white sport jacket with a wild purple ruffled shirt. Wow! What a site that was! That was the style back then!

We arrived at the dance, found ourselves a table and proceeded to have a great time.

The dance hall was decorated with a large crystal ball, hanging in the middle of the dance floor, with spot lights of different colors pointing at it causing a sensational looking strobe light.

It was a bring your own bottle event, so I took along a bottle of sloe gin, a favorite drink the wife liked at the time, and a fifth of Jim Beam for myself and Dan.

We had a wonderful time of dancing, talking and drinking the evening away.

When we were leaving, much later that night, Dan was in a great mood and about half crocked. I wouldn't say he was drunk, but I could tell he was feeling no pain. Needless to say, I was feeling pretty good myself and was glad I wasn't the one doing the driving. The wife and I got in the back seat and just settled in for the ride back home. We had just backed out of our parking space and started to leave. That is when the trouble began.

As we were leaving, there were two or three guys and their women walking in the middle of the parking lot, probably going to their cars. They were hanging onto each other probably trying to hold each other up; I just could not tell which. Dan was slowly coming up behind them in the car and being half drunk himself, began blowing the horn at them just for the fun of it.

I guess Dan must have pissed a couple of the guys off because they got mad that he was blowing the horn.

I believe a couple of these fellows tried to impress their wives or girlfriends by trying to punch Dan out by reaching through the window of his car. Dan, being a pretty good size fellow, just leaned over to avoid the punches, laughing even more.

At first, the wife and I thought these guys were just fooling around. We were just sitting there waiting for them to end their "fun" when all of a sudden the back door opens on my side of the car. I should have had the dang thing locked! This guy proceeds to reach in and grab hold of me, pulling me out of the car!

When this unknown assailant pulled me from the car, he tore the collar off my shirt, which pissed me off real good!

I landed on my hands and knees in the graveled parking lot with these two guys beating me on the back of my head and shoulders. What they did not know, however, is that I had grabbed the bottle of sloe gin when I exited the car! When I was able to stand up, I clobbered the first guy nearest to me; right in the face with that bottle of sloe gin.

I guess I must have busted his nose pretty good as a lot of blood began to fly. The guy's girlfriend ran up to me, yelling in my face about her boyfriend. He was rolling around, clutching his face, and bleeding all over everything.

I told the gal that if she didn't want some of the same thing I gave him, she'd better get out of my face. Needless to say, everybody else took off when they saw the damage to their buddy's face.

Dan and I got back into the car and started to leave again when this guy jumps up and begins running alongside the car. He was punching the window trying to hit me while cursing and yelling.

Dan was driving about five miles an hour when this guy who was running alongside the car, tripped over his own feet and rolled head over heels injuring himself even more! Finally we were able to leave the parking lot. On our way home, we passed an ambulance headed toward the Crystal Ball.

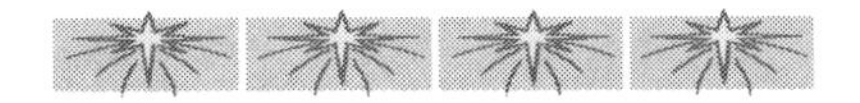

I suspect to administer first aid to the guy that I had hit with the bottle and to the injuries he created to himself when he fell alongside the car.

I took a picture of the car the next day as there was blood all over the side of the car. Dan and I washed the car after I took the pictures and we never did hear anymore about the incident again. We never went back to the Crystal Ball after that either!

We thought that if you had to fight your way out of a place, it just was not worth going to.

RECOGNIZED

At the time I was attending the Miami County Police Academy; a deputy from Miami County recognized my name and remembered that I had been in the county jail for "something." This deputy told the chief of police that I was attending the police academy and that I could not be a police officer in the state of Ohio because of a previous conviction.

I then received a letter from the mayor and village council of Versailles, dated February 9, 1976 that my services were no longer needed and I was terminated. I was given no explanation or reason, but in my heart I knew why.

This was when I contacted Attorney Thomas Hanes from Greenville, Ohio. I requested his help in finding out if I had any legal remedies that could or would help my cause in keeping my legal writes afforded me by law.

My attorney checked the Ohio Revised Code and found that at the termination of my five years of probation, I was restored all of my rights as a resident of the state of Ohio. There were no known legal reasons why I could not be a police officer.

My attorney wrote a letter to the village council and Mayor stating this information. The village "powers" would not change their minds, but did agree to allow me to finish the police academy since it was already paid for.

Mr. Hanes found out that Ohio legislatures had passed legislation effective January 1, 1974, allowing under certain conditions, that my previous conviction could be expunged under section 2953.32 of the Ohio Revised Code.

On February 17, 1976 I applied to the Miami County Common Pleas Court to expunge my previous conviction that occurred on the ninth day of May, 1963.

While attending the police academy, I had met and become friends with the chief of police of Mechanicsburg, Ohio. I told the chief that the village of Versailles had let me go and also told him why.

I let him read the letter from my attorney stating that I could be a police officer and that he had filed a motion with the courts to have my past conviction expunged.

It was shortly after being terminated from the Versailles, Ohio police department that Chief Moore asked me to do some undercover surveillance for him at the Mechanicsburg City Park. Chief Moore said he felt that there were drugs being sold there.

DATE OF COM. 7-24-76

DATE OF BIRTH 2-I7-43

HT. 5 - II WT. I90

HAIR Brn. EYES Hazl.

Sgt Gary D. Goffinet

SIGNATURE

THIS CARD IS THE PROPERTY OF THE VILLAGE OF MECHANICSBURG AND MUST BE SURRENDERED UPON REQUEST OF THE CHIEF OF POLICE.

EXPIRATION DATE Indeft.

MECHANICSBURG, OHIO

I told the chief that if he could get me hired as a part time police officer at one dollar per year (known as an auxiliary officer), I would be glad to help him out. Chief Moore talked to the Mayor and on February 10, 1976, I was sworn in as a part time police officer with the Mechanicsburg, Ohio police department. I began working a covert operation for the Mechanicsburg Police Department while waiting for the courts to hear my expungement case.

I began watching the city park from a field with a small hill overlooking it. I was watching the park during the evening, when most of the illegal activity occurred. After a short time, I was able to get pictures and license plate numbers off of the vehicles I thought were coming to the park on a regular basis. These were the same vehicles that the suspected druggies congregated around.

My sister-in-law Diane came with me a few times to help out with notes and such. She said she was a little interested in becoming an undercover cop. She never followed up on that venture.

While I was working the undercover job for Chief Moore, I finished the Ohio Peace Officer Criminal Code Training Program on the 7th day of April 1976 and finished the Ohio Police Basic Law Enforcement

Officer Training Program on the 12th day of April of the same year.

On March 22, 1976 I appeared in Miami County Common Pleas Court with my Attorney, Mr. Hanes. The Court ordered all official records pertaining to case no. 8475, to be sealed and all references thereto, be deleted.

I still did not receive my Official Certificate during my time with the Mechanicsburg Department for "whatever reason". I just kept on trying to accomplish my goal: to be a Police Officer.

On July 12, 1977, I wrote a letter to the Ohio Peace Officers Training Council at the direction of my attorney, requesting the specific reasons for their refusal to issue my certification. I told them that I could obtain employment much easier if I had proof that I had completed the proper training.

I went back to Versailles to say hello to some of my friends and just visit for awhile. I told Officer Cool that I had gotten a police job in Mechanicsburg, Ohio and showed him my badge. Later on, that was when he showed his true colors.

On February 10, 1976 Officer Tom Cool, (who was the acting Chief of Police due to the beating of Chief Frantz) wrote me a wonderful recommendation that I included in my resume's to different Police Departments.

After I was hired on as an auxiliary officer in

Mechanicsburg, Officer Cool took it upon himself to call Chief Wayne Moore asking if I indeed was working as a police officer with badge #10. When Chief Moore confirmed that fact, Officer Cool immediately called the Champaign County Sheriff, spilling his guts about everything he knew about me.

Then Sheriff Roger Stilling called Chief Moore and told him the very same thing that Officer Cool had just told him minutes earlier, adding that I was a convicted felon and could not be a police officer in the state of Ohio. This act told me that Officer Cool was no friend of mine except to my face!

While I was working with the Mechanicsburg Police Dept, I made many friends while making a number of cases on a few drug dealers. I captured a fellow who had escaped from the Ohio Penitentiary and had eluded police officers for two years!

Two incidents come to mind that was significant while I was with this police department.

One was when The Ohio Grain Company blew up killing a customer and injuring three others.

There were only three full time police officers on the department during this time and it was really hard trying to keep people back from the scene. One of the bystanders actually stepped on the dead man's eyeball!

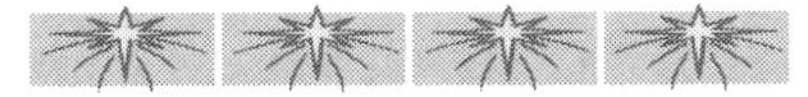

A huge steel door had hit the customer in the head with such force that his eyeball exploded from his face. The bystander actually began throwing up when he saw the guy's eye stuck to his shoe.

Then, at the next village council meeting, the fire Chief Dick Chester spent quite some time criticizing Chief Moore for not properly controlling the crowds at the scene of the explosion. But! Mr. Chester expressed appreciation to other groups and agencies for their help! What Dick didn't realize was; Chief Moore was the one who put out the call for assistance because he knew his department was short handed!

As I remember in late May 1977, a village citizen, Mr. Ed Moore complained at the village council meeting that there were no police coverage on Sundays or early morning hours during the week and wanted to know why. Chief Moore explained that with a three man force it was nearly impossible to cover the village twenty four hours a day. He was however, putting officers on duty during the hours he thought were most active by people who were committing crimes.

The Mayor, at the time; Mr. Frank Gregg, advised Chief Moore that he must use his officer's more efficiently during peak crime hours. I personally felt that he was! You can only cover so many hours with so many officers!

AN ATTEMPTED KILL

The second incident brought me to understand how easily it was for someone to try to kill a police officer.

It was a quite Friday evening and during "my rounds" I always lock the gate to the local cemetery. I checked to make sure there were no visitors visiting their lost loved ones. I stopped at the entrance gate to lock it up for the night.

As the cruiser stopped, my clipboard slid off the seat onto the floorboard. I leaned over to retrieve it when the "still of the night" was broken by gunfire!

Small particles of glass flew around the inside of the cruiser. Luckily, because I was leaning over, I only received some nicks and scratches to the side of my face. I thank the Lord to this day, for windshields made of safety glass and for causing my clipboard to slide off the seat!

I crawled across the seat and got out of the car on the passenger's side as to not give the assailant any further chance of seeing me in the drivers' location. I opened the door and staying behind it, I got out with my side arm "at the ready" to defend myself from whoever was trying to kill me.

As I looked out between the door and the cruiser's body, I observed someone running up the road away from the cemetery. I could have possibly got a shot off but then realized that the houses at the end of the road were in the line of fire. I just would not take the chance of endangering innocent people.

I rushed around the vehicle to the driver's seat thinking I'd give chase. A split second later, I thought maybe the person might be waiting for me so I just called for backup.

It was just a few short minutes and there were deputies from the sheriffs department and Chief Moore on the scene trying to find the person who had taken a shot at me. They found no one around but when the BCI (Bureau of Criminal Investigation) investigators got there, they found the wadding from a 12 gauge shotgun with number six shot. They said it had to have been a single shot firearm.

To this day this shooting has never been solved. I suspect that the person is still hunting me or it was just a random act by someone who was pissed off at the police for some unknown reason.

The chief called me on Sunday morning of June 12, 1977, stating that he had received a complaint of a person riding a motorcycle up and down the sidewalk on Walnut Street, and ask me to go check it out.

I parked about a half block away and approached the area on foot. I hid behind a row of hedges and watched as the rider lined up the motorcycle and launched it down the sidewalk at an incredible rate of speed! I could only guess the speed to be in excess of sixty miles an hour!

I stepped out from behind the bush row and observed the rider that I knew as Kevin O'Brien. When he saw me, he rode his bike into his garage which was only a few yards from where I was standing. I asked him for his driver's license and the registration to the motorcycle.

He came from his garage and approached me with his helmet in hand and forcibly hit me in the chest with it telling me to get off his property. I told him that I was going to cite him to court for disturbing the peace and I still wanted to see his papers. When he approached me the second time in a threatening manner, I hit him with my slapstick striking the left side of his head, across his ear.

He spun around and tried to "bulldog" me with his head down (as a charging bull would). I hit him again with the slapjack, this time taking him to the ground. After I handcuffed him, I called for an ambulance because the blood was running from the top of his head down to his face. It looked worse than it really was, but try to tell that to a bunch of people who had quickly gathered around. The ambulance arrived and took Kevin to the hospital where he received a couple of stitches and was sent home.

After disbursing the scene, I went to the police station to finish up all the paperwork.

I had just begun to put together the day's events when I was interrupted by two gentlemen who angrily entered the police station. Mr. Robert O'Brien and Mr. Bill Rutan wanted to speak with me.

Mr. O'Brien, the father of Kevin, whom I had just arrested, was standing there very pissed off at me. He threatened to get me fired and if that didn't work, he would personally take care of me some other way.

I told Bob that it would be in his best interest to go home and cool off before he got himself into more trouble than he needed. He left the station saying, "You have not heard the last of this."

It was very soon after this incident, (maybe two days) that Chief Moore told me that the Village Safety Committee wanted me on desk duty beginning June 12, 1977. I was restricted from my normal patrol functions for a while for my safety and to let the town cool down. This was normal procedure.

I began seeing the "hand writing on the wall." My position with the Mechanicsburg Police Department was going to end soon as the pressure mounted on the Mayor and the Chief of Police to get rid of me. This pressure was also coming from other councilmen and citizens who themselves were involved in other "not so legal" activities.

These other citizens knew that I was always investigating complaints from law abiding people and could possibly turn up at their door with a search warrant or a warrant for their arrest! I truly believe this was the real reason the council wanted me gone!

Chief Moore was, in my opinion, the best supervisor I had ever worked for in my career as a police officer. He taught me a lot in the field of law enforcement and about life in general.

After he and I spoke about the pressure he was under in reference to my job, I tendered my resignation from the police department to the Mayor on June 23, 1977. I resigned because I wanted to defend him as the Chief, a colleague and very good friend of mine.

Later I found out that the Ohio Peace Officer Training Council was refusing to issue my certification because I should not have been allowed to finish the school. But, due do to the fact that I had finished the school, they would issue my certification upon receiving verification that I had received a commission as a police officer from a City or Village in the state of Ohio.

During the time the negotiations were going on between me and the Ohio Peace Officers Training Council, I was working for Henrys Gas Station in Mechanicsburg, pumping gas and towing vehicles that needed repair.

Certificate of Completion and Competency

DOPPLER RADAR OPERATION

Ptl. Gary D. Goffinet

NAME AND TITLE

of the Covington, Oh. Police Dept

DEPARTMENT

has successfully completed a course of instruction in the use and operation of Doppler Radar and is deemed competent to utilize Doppler Radar to determine the velocity of motor vehicles.

Further; He has exhibited the capability of instructing others in the skill.

10-6-77

DATE

TRAINING REPRESENTATIVE
DECATUR ELECTRONICS, INC
DECATUR, ILLINOIS

COVINGTON, OHIO

I finally was hired on with the Covington, Ohio Police Dept as a Patrolman. Mayor Donald Garman wrote a letter to the Ohio Peace Officers Training Council confirming my commission as a full time police officer on August 31, 1977.

On September 9, 1977 I received my certificate which was seventeen months after I had completed the schooling! I had been working as a police officer nearly the whole time.

I began patrolling the streets of Covington as a regular patrol officer. I also was certified to operate the Doppler speed radar gun that the department used for clocking speeders. I issued many, many speeding and other citations to mayor's court.

The senior citizens of Covington had what they call "seniors day." That year they decided to have a "mock" mayor's court. I actually made the newspaper by acting like Clem Kiddelhopper in their mock mayor's court! I also made the paper during the girls Tri-Hi-Y powder puff football game! Herman "Moose" Osborn, representing the Covington Fire Department and myself, representing the Police Department, showed up at the football game dressed like cheer leaders! We were an instant "hit" with the school kids!

When I was hired, the Chief of Police was Norman R. Miller. He retired shortly thereafter and Billie Joe Ray replaced him as Chief of Police.

It took me some time to figure out why my job was to come to an end in Covington. The mystery was solved when I found out that Mr. Ray was the chief probation officer for Miami County before he applied for the position of Chief of Police in Covington.

This gave him access to all the records in that department and that is where he found the information in regards to my being convicted of a crime. He did not ask me if I had my record expunged or anything about me being totally legal in my position as a police officer.

He just decided to use whatever means he could to see to it that I did not receive my confirmation after a probationary time of six months. After six months of perfect attendance, writing more citations than all other officers on the department combined, and working traffic in minus zero weather during the blizzard of 1977-1978, I received a letter of termination on Feb 27, 1978.

I found out later "from sources" that he was just making a position for a good friend of his who was a Darke County deputy sheriff at the time.

That came back to bite him in the ass because the Deputy that Chief Ray hired, was arrested on October18, 1978 by the F.B.I. for his part in robbing the Arcanum National Bank in Arcanum, Ohio! **IMAGINE THAT, REPLACING ME WITH A BANK ROBBER!**

The bank robbery took place on March 20, 1978, and the "bank robber" was hired by Covington, Ohio police department in April of the same year! Guess they didn't check him out very well!

SHE

WORKERS COMPENSATION CASES

I continued working private investigations for various departments. I also worked for a private investigation firm out of Troy, Ohio owned by my friend Jack Cheadle.

I worked for Jack as an armed security guard for a company in Jackson Center, Ohio called Plastic Pac, and investigated workers compensation fraud cases.

A co-worker and I followed these people around and videotaped them working, while at the same time, drawing workers compensation from the State of Ohio

One story comes to mind as I'm writing. This is another time I was actually shot at during my work in the law enforcement field.

Mr. Cheadle's son and I were watching this person working on a construction job. He was digging a hole by hand! Now that's hard work and labor intensive!

We were in a van with a one way glass, watching and taking pictures of this guy. All of a sudden he whips out a firearm from his tool box and he's approaching the van, yelling obscenities!

We took off in the van while the guy was either shooting in the air or he was just not a good shot because he never did hit us or the van! When we got back to the office, we could not find any bullet holes in the van. Yep! He must have been a bad shot!

While doing all of this, I continued looking for a police position with any village or town that may be hiring.

With the help of one of the part time agents on the department, I got a job with Leroy Dresser Industries in Sidney, Ohio.

My family and I moved from Covington back to the home we owned in Mechanicsburg, Ohio as it was much more cost effective for us. While I worked as a machine setup person for Dresser Industries, I continued keeping close contact with police officers that I attended the police academy with in hopes of getting a lead on a new police job.

Chief Moore was still a good friend and he was giving me information on departments that was looking for police officers. I took a part time job with the West Manchester, Ohio police department and just worked on Friday and Saturday nights. This kept my certification good and enabled me to continue looking for a full time position.

My wife and I became good friends with one of the local police officers that Mechanicsburg had hired in my absence. We use to sit around and play cards. This officer, Bradley, was just too damn nice for his own good. He allowed people to get away with things they should not have gotten away with.

The Mechanicsburg Police Department finally let him go. See! It doesn't even pay to be "nice" in this line of work! You are damned if you do and damned if you don't.

A short time later he came to my house saying the town he grew up around was looking to hire a whole new police department. They had fired all of the officers they had and Bradley was unsure as to why. His uncle was on the village council and he felt that we could get the job if we wanted it.

At this time I had been laid off from Dresser Industries and was drawing unemployment. I thought, why not! It was worth a try and it was full time work!

So in midsummer, we loaded up our eighteen foot travel trailer and headed for the beautiful scenic county of Adams County, Ohio and the Village of Manchester, to check on these police positions.

Bradley got the chief's job with the help of his uncle, and I helped him to set up the department. I set up a dispatching center, got some file cabinets and started a filing system.

We went to the village clerk's office to find out what the police departments annual budget was. We needed to know if we could hire any more officers and if so, how many.

The first obstacle we came to was the officers from the previous department had a lawsuit filed against the village. They claimed that they were union members and could not be terminated because of their union contract.

The chief, (Bradley) could not be confirmed as a full time chief until the lawsuit was settled. This was not a major issue because Ohio law says that a newly hired officer had to work a six months probationary period before he could be confirmed as a full time certified officer. So the village had six months to get the lawsuit settled before Bradley's confirmation period would come up.

On June 23, 1980, Bradley Bilyeu started his job as Chief of Police and a few days later I was sworn in as a part time officer at one dollar per year. This was ok with me because I was still drawing unemployment at the time.

Manchester was the only "wet" village in Adams County. The town had its share of people drinking and driving, fighting and other crimes. There were eleven places to obtain or drink alcoholic beverages in this village of thirty nine hundred people.

The department had its hands full, since Bradley and I were the only ones who were covering this small town of drunken rednecks, construction workers, and riverboat workers.

In a very short time the jewelry store had been broken into and eleven hundred dollars worth of merchandise was stolen and damage to the store was extensive. Then the local drug store was robbed and a large quantity of drugs was taken.

The village council began giving the chief a hard time saying that he was not spending enough time patrolling the town and covering the streets as they thought he should.

Between the chief and me we spent well over one hundred twenty five hours a week patrolling and fighting crime. Two officers could not be 'on the streets" twenty four hours a day seven days a week! We also had a family and a home life that we were attempting to maintain in a comfortable manner.

Chief Bilyeu was doing all he could to maintain the peace in town. What he seemed to lack was the enthusiasm that it took to deal with all the problems.

About the same time that Bradley and I were hired, the Dayton Power and Light Company began building a new generation station on the Ohio River just a few miles outside of town. This drew in hundreds of construction workers from all over the country.

The village of Manchester, being the only 'wet' town in Adams County, had beer joints and carry outs but did not have a hotel within miles. We had people living in campers, tents, cars, and trucks. After awhile, some of the women that were on welfare would take guys in because of love or money, who knows!

Friday and Saturday nights were a total disaster. We were arresting people for drunk and disorderly conduct, public intoxication, driving while under the influence and many other crimes related to alcohol that you can imagine.

Then came the complaints from some of the village council members, again. They claimed we were running business from town by arresting people. We were accused of sitting outside of the bars waiting on people to come out and then arresting them. That claim was so far from the truth that I could not believe the village council would even believe such a thing!

The fact was that a couple of council members owned the bars or had relatives that did. Even the ex mayor owned one of the local carryouts.

So, it became a regular discussion at every council meeting in reference to the "events" of the police department. How many people did we arrest? How many people did we stop for speeding? You name it, we were questioned about it.

Then the only hardware store in the town burned down. Everyone thought it was just a fire till Chief Bilyeu and I proved it was arson. Now the fire Chief was great at running the fire department but did not have a clue when it came to investigating crimes.

He disagreed with us until the owner of the hardware store came to a council meeting and confirmed he had lost several tools: including three or four chain saws, power saws, electric drills and other small tools from the break in and fire.

These items were not among the burnt items, so they had to have been stolen!

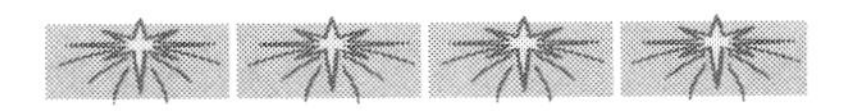

Chief Bilyeu lived in his father's home about five miles from town near the small village of Rome, Ohio. The village council decided that they wanted the police officers who were full time, to live within the village limits. This meant Bradley would have to move to town.

Chief Bilyeu was living at his dad's house rent free, making it easier for him to live on the nine thousand dollar salary that the village was paying him. He found himself in a dilemma. Either move to town where there was no affordable place to rent or resign from the department. After considering all the problems the council had given him and the fact he did not want to move to town, Bradley resigned from the department in early September, 1980.

On September 3rd of the same year, Bradley and I were both sworn in as Adams County Deputy Sheriffs. We began patrolling Adams County in our new capacities as county deputy sheriffs.

POLICE OFFICER
MANCHESTER, OHIO 45144
JURISDICTION, STATE
NAME Gary D. Goffinet
SIGNATURE Gary D. Goffinet
2/43 6' 200 HZL BRN M
DATE ISSUED September 16, 1980
ISSUED BY Mayor Ed Gilkison
TITLE Chief Gary Goffinet

MANCHESTER, OHIO

On September 16, 1980, I received a call from Mayor Ed Gilkison asking me to come to town to speak with him.

I went to town and he asks me to take the position of Chief of Police with a salary of ten thousand dollars per year. He would give me the six month probationary period to move to town if I agreed to the position.

I went to the Sheriff's Office and resigned from my part time position as a deputy. At this time (1980) in the State of Ohio, you could not hold two different police commissions at the same time.

I went back to Manchester and was sworn in as the Chief of Police by Mayor Edward Gilkison. I began my duties by setting up the department the way I wanted it set up.

Almost from the beginning I ran into some difficulties with some of the "union" officers who had been let go much earlier. They were demanding their jobs back!

Later in the month, the village council voted to reinstate Ms. Carol Jones and Mr. Francis Bowman. I was ask to notify them of the council's decision and to find out when they could return to work.

Ms. Jones explained to me that at the present time she could only work day shift because she had children to care for.

This created a little problem since I only had three full time officers including myself. I let Carol know that I firmly believed that my officers should get to know all the residents of a town and the only way to do that was to work all three shifts at one time or another.

When it came time for Officer Jones to work the four o'clock to midnight shifts, she right away went to her favorite councilman and cried to him. Carol felt she should not have to work that shift because all the drunks would be out and she could not handle those situations.

Her "favorite" councilman approached me later and questioned me as to why I was going to schedule a lady officer to work the night shift? I simply told him that all of my officers would work the shift in question and I was even going to do the same. I also advised him that Ohio law gives the police chief the sole authority on who works where in his department and that Ms. Jones had the same police training as all other officers in regards to doing her job.

I advised Officer Jones that if she needed assistance, she had a radio and could call for help at any time to either Officer Bowman or myself.

Officer Jones was a robust women about six foot tall and around two hundred forty five pounds. She started calling me or Officer Bowman out of bed just because she could not seem to handle the activities on any given Friday or Saturday night. The local taverns had fights, stabbings, and shootings almost every Friday and Saturday night.

I still remember the night when Carol knocked on my door about two o'clock in the early morning hours, in tears. She said that Rocky Bradford (a local trouble maker) was at his house, on the front porch, playing his radio so loud that the neighbors were calling the police department and complaining.

On her arrival to his house, she found Rocky to be highly intoxicated and very obnoxious. Rocky told her to get her fat ass off his property.

I asked her if she asked him to turn the volume down on his radio and to be more polite to his neighbors. She told me she had made that request and he replied with "get your fat ass off my property."

I got my uniform on and upon arrival to Mr. Bradford's home, I found him still playing his radio at a high volume and still on the porch raising hell.

At this time I was carrying a Buford stick that I had fashioned after the movie "Walking Tall." I stepped upon to the porch and in one swift swing; I crushed the stupid radio and told Rocky that if I had to come back again he would spend the rest of the weekend in the county jail.

Needless to say, there were no more calls to that residence for the rest of the weekend.

There were so many events happening during this period, that I probably could write a whole book on this town alone. With eleven bars and carryouts and being the only "wet" town in the county, the writings would never end!

A short time after Officer Bowman was rehired, he began telling me about different people in town who were trouble makers and had to be approached very cautiously. He told me of one fellow by the name of Charley Manchester, could be a real problem if I encountered him while he was drunk. He supposedly has fought about every cop in the county at one time or another. Officer Bowman added that Charley's wife, Billie was a very small lady who could whip two grown men by herself if she got in a fight with them.

It was a couple of months later that I was running radar on the east side of town. It was a late evening on a warm Friday in mid July, when a vehicle coming towards me was traveling at fifty eight miles per hour in a thirty five mile per hour zone.

I stopped the car just at the village limits and went through the normal procedure. I ask the driver for his operator's license and the registration to the vehicle. As the driver (who was by himself) was retrieving his paperwork from various areas of the vehicle, I smelled a very strong odor of alcohol emitting from his opened window. When the man gave me his paperwork, he was talking with very slurred speech assuring me that he was in fact, intoxicated.

When I looked at his operator's license, I recognized the name Charley Manchester and knew then that I had encountered the guy that Officer Bowman had told me about earlier.

With this knowledge at the forefront of my brain, I asked Mr. Manchester to wait in the car. I went back to my patrol car, took off my gun belt and uniform shirt and put them on the front seat. I proceeded back to the car where Charley was waiting. As I approached the car, I told Charley that I had been told by other officers that if I ever encountered him, I would have to fight him. I told Charley that if we were going to fight, then he needed to get out of the car and let's get this fight over with. I told him whatever the outcome of the fight was: win lose or draw, he was the one who would be going to jail for the weekend. Or! He could let me do my job and I would see to it that he would get to go home that night.

After a few seconds of thought, Charley said to me, "Ok, I will just see how good you are at keeping your word Chief." He got out of his car, allowed me to handcuff him, and place him in the patrol car without any problem at all. I took him to the county sheriff's office where he took the breathalyzer test. Charley flunked the test and tested .18% which was eight points higher than the legal limit. I wrote Charley a citation for speeding and one for driving under the influence of alcohol. I advised him of his court date and how much the bond would be if he elected to post bond.

Charley then said to me, "I guess you are now going to lock me up for the weekend, right Chief?" And I told him that I was a man of my word and I was taking him home, just as I said I would.

The deputies at the Sheriff's Office told me that I was making a big mistake by taking him home. I told them it was my choice and I was taking him home as promised.

When we arrived at his house, I knocked on the door. When his wife answered the door, she was in total disbelief that I had brought him home. I asked her and Charley one favor that night: and that was for them to stay home till Charley was sober then come to town the next day and pick up his car, which they complied.

I was a police officer in Adams County for a long time after that and never had the first problem with Charlie or his wife again.

In reality, I had more problems with some of the village council people than I ever had with the citizens of Manchester, Ohio.

A couple of the council people sat around listening to their police scanners so they could count how many vehicles I stopped on any given night. I would then be accused of running a speed trap and running business out of town.

Of course one of the councilmen in question owned two of the local taverns in town. Business must have been down at his place!

Over the next six months there were many incidents that happened because most people had gotten accustomed to not having a police presence around. The citizens were just doing whatever they wanted, legal or not! Naturally this would cause conflict between law abiding and non-law abiding citizens.

I was hired to enforce the laws of the State of Ohio and the laws and ordinances of the village of Manchester, and that was just what I was doing, whether the councilmen liked it or not!

One of the incidents included me making a felony arrest. Unlike all of the other citations I issued, this one was different in that it was a felony.

It was June of 1981 when I learned about a felony warrant on a guy who lived in our town. I was surprised that the Sheriff's Department had not picked this guy up a long time ago! I verified that the warrant was still active and proceeded to find this guy.

It only took two days after word got out on the streets. I had a good relationship with the kids in town and they are the ones who found this felony offender for me!

I called in Officer Bowman and Auxiliary Officer Don Bradford as back-up. We arrived at his house and arrested him without incident.

HOOVER MEMORIAL AWARD

NATIONALY RECOGNIZED

It was during the same summer that I was notified by my dispatcher to be on the lookout for a vehicle with California tags that was headed in my direction. These suspects were wanted for a couple of armed robberies and a shooting in Cincinnati, Ohio.

I was at home at the time the call came in, so I put on my uniform and went to my patrol car. I proceeded to the first intersection which was about twenty five yards from my driveway. I stopped at the stop sign to wait for an oncoming car and low and behold it was the very car that I was told to be on the lookout for!

It was uncanny as hell! I fell in behind the car with California tags and began following it. I also radioed the county telling them what I was doing and they needed to send a backup unit just in case I needed help.

I observed three subjects in the car. The county radioed to tell me there was a couple of units close by. I stopped the vehicle and ordered the suspects out of the car with my twelve gauge shotgun. I made them lay on their bellies in the road and waited for my backup to arrive.

After the other officers arrived, we searched each one, handcuffed them and placed them in the patrol car for transport to the county jail. The vehicle was searched and a Browning forty five automatic pistol was found under the passenger's seat.

After finding the weapon, I was thankful that I used all the proper procedures in making this stop as it could have been much worse if a shooting situation had happened.

Later that year I was notified that I had been nominated to receive the National Police Officer Award of the Year for the State of Ohio. I was also chosen to receive the John Edgar Hoover Memorial Police Service award.

I was presented the award in May of the next year by the Judge of the county. My parents attended this ceremony and the party afterwards. That was the last time I had gotten so-o-o-o drunk. There was an article in the National Chiefs of Police Magazine regarding my award. This article put the Village of Manchester in the national news: probably the only time in the town's history.

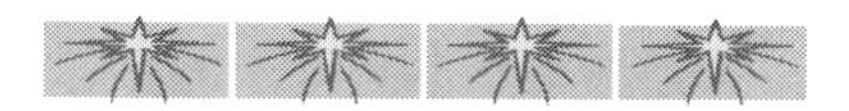

It was still an uphill climb being the Chief of Police in Manchester. A few of the council members continued their pursuit of trying to run the police department or getting rid of it entirely.

I still remember nights when they actually tried

following our patrol cars with their lights off! That just goes to show how stupid they were.

Officer Bradford and I would fill our gas tanks as full as we could, then drive up and down every street and alley in town just to make them use up their gas. Then we got this great idea! Don and I cleaned out his dad's garage so we could get a car in it. One night while on patrol, we knew that one of the councilmen was following us. After driving for a short period of time, we cut down an alley and put the patrol car in the garage and closed the door. Then we would do foot patrol while they drove up and down the streets looking for us. It was hilarious.

MOVING ON

I finally got my belly full of the statements and innuendos about: where were you? who did you arrest? and being told certain people (like their relatives) should be left alone to do as they pleased. I went to the mayor and told him I was resigning and he needed to find himself someone else to fill the Chief's job.

He questioned me as to the reason and I told him that certain councilmen were making my job just too stressful. I was tired of them threatening me with my job.

Now Ed was a great mayor and told me he understood as they did the same thing to him all the time. He told me that most all of the business owners in town really liked me and would hate to see me leave. They knew their stores were in good hands when it was closed. The mayor said he felt that I had done a whale of a job and I would be missed by most.

During my tenure at Manchester, Ohio I had kept in close contact with Mr. Jack Cheadle. Remember him? He was the owner of a private investigation firm. I called him asking if he had any security work or investigations that he would like me to participate in. I let him know that I had resigned from the Chiefs job in Manchester.

He told me to come see him because he had a few jobs in mind that he thought I could handle.

I drove to his office in Troy, Ohio and we discussed me working in Logan County, Ohio in a covert drug investigation. He wanted to introduce me to the Prosecutors investigator for Logan County and to determine exactly what it was that he had in mind.

In the meantime I took a part time position with the Seaman, Ohio police department so I could keep my certification current. The chief of police in Seaman was Chief Wayne Baldwin. Wayne and I belonged to the Adams County Police Officers Association and I knew him from working on some burglary investigations in Adams County. Wayne was having much better luck than I did in running his department. The mayor and council allowed him to run the department as he deemed necessary. Wayne was also a "hometown" boy, if you know what I mean. Wayne had no problem getting me approved by the council and I was sworn in by Mayor Carl Musser.

So I added another police job to my list of places I worked as a police officer in the state of Ohio.

I went to Bellefontaine, Ohio with Jack and met with the prosecutors' investigator to set up the covert operation they wanted me to do.

The job was pretty routine. I was to rid the county of the drug dealers and solve some of the bigger crimes in Logan County.

Sometimes it was just unbelievable to me how far people would go to screw with somebody. I thought Manchester was in my past! But no! One of the village councilmen actually wrote a letter to the place in Columbus, Ohio where we bought our uniforms and other police related equipment.

He had requested a list of every piece of equipment that I had purchased from them during my tenure as Chief of Police!

They in turn called me and informed me about the request. I told them to go ahead and send the list to him. I had nothing to hide!

The councilmen probably thought that I had purchased something for the village and had taken it with me when I resigned. I knew that these kind of things happened with these kind of people.

When I left the department, I made sure that the Village Clerk and I counted every piece of inventory the police department was suppose to have. I'm a firm believer in CYA. Cover Your A_ _!

When the councilman checked the inventory he found that everything was in order. I thought that was going to satisfy his ego to somehow pin something on me. I was wrong! He questioned the dispatchers about various things and one of them (whose name is not worth mentioning) told him that I had removed all of the records from the Chief's office! The next thing I knew, Officer Bowman was at my door telling me that the councilman ordered him to come get the departments records from me or they would get a court order. I informed Officer Bowman that I did not have what they were asking for and if they truly thought I did; go get a court order!

Just a few days later I received a call from Judge Elliot Bucher, the Common Pleas Judge of Adams County. The judge requested that I bring the paperwork to his office so he could see what this councilman was talking about. I complied with the judge's request. He saw that the records in question were MY records and that I had a receipt where I had paid for them.

I explained to the judge what was going on and he assured me that this problem would be stopped.

I never heard another thing from Manchester, Ohio again.

LOGAN COUNTY

I was sworn in as a Special Deputy Sheriff in Logan County, Ohio and was preparing to start the covert investigation that we had discussed earlier.

Jack introduced me to a guy who was supposed to be some sort of informant who knew every bad ass in Logan County. He was supposed to get me into places where drugs and gambling were going on. After two nights, I knew this guy did not know crap and was just blowing smoke up Jack's butt.

The second night, we were downtown sitting on a street bench when five or six patrol cars came by with people in the back seats. Most all of them looked to be very young people but Bobby freaked out! He began saying that we had "been made" and we needed to get out of town! I told him to go ahead and leave if he wished but I thought he was full of crap and I was staying because I could see no problem.

Bobby left town and I started setting up the operation the way I felt would work the best for me.

I called Jack and informed him about my feelings in reference to Bobby and not to bother sending any other stupid confidential informants to help me out as I could get along fine without them. From that time on, I always refused to work with a partner.

I began by renting a motel room and getting my "props" set up, so as to lead people to believe that it was a real construction company. This "construction company" was preparing to add an addition on to the Honda Manufacturing plant in Marysville, Ohio.

In a covert operation, your props are everything if you want people to think you are who you're pretending to be. Props make your story totally believable. The company I set up was called Sunbelt Contractors out of Addison, Texas.

I put an ad in the local newspaper for construction workers needed i.e.: carpenters, laborers, painters, concrete workers, etc. They were to apply at room twenty two at The Holiday Inn between the hours of 10 am to 4 pm, Wednesday through Friday on given dates at that time.

People began showing up and putting in applications for the various positions. They ask all kinds of questions about what kind of tools they would need, how much the pay would be and when will the job break ground.

I informed all of them they would need the tools that they normally used in their respective craft; the pay started at fifteen dollars and fifty cents per hour and would top out at about eighteen dollars per hour, as the job progressed.

In the time I took applications, I received between twenty five and thirty applications that I thought would be good leads to finding people who could get me some pot or other type of illegal drugs.

In the meantime, I moved our house trailer from Manchester to Seaman, Ohio when I was hired on as a police officer there. I was working the covert operation from my home on Sundays and Mondays, as it was some distance from home to the area where I was working undercover.

I also worked on Sundays and Mondays as a regular police officer for the village. I did whatever needed to be done to give the Chief some well needed time off.

I would go to Logan County on Tuesday evening. I stayed in a small house that I rented using money supplied to me by the county.

This covert operation lasted about seven months and I thought it was going very well. I made sixty three separate purchases of suspected controlled substances such as pot, speed, downers, acid, cocaine and heroin. I got two women to sell me a "lay in the hay" and seven pieces of stolen property.

The total number of defendant's indicted were twenty one on a total of seventy seven separate charges against them.

During this covert operation I ran into very little problems but there was just a couple that could have turned bad for me and the operation.

A young girl, whom I had befriended, was giving me all kinds of leads on who was selling different kinds of pills, pot and other stuff. I will call the young girl, Amy.

She was downtown and heard a guy by the name of Ralph telling someone that he thought I was a narc. She called me right away telling me I should be careful when I come back to town because people would be really pissed.

When I arrived back in the county I went straight to Ralph's house where I found him out in his yard with another fellow. I asked him to take a short ride with me.

I took him to Russell's Point, which is near Indian Lake State Park and proceeded to kick the crap out of him, and said: "I was going to kill your ass and dump your body in the lake for the fish to eat, go to your house and do your old lady and then burn your house down!!"

He was on his knees begging me to stop kicking him, asking me why I was so pissed off at him. I explained to him that I had gotten word that he had been running his mouth and saying he thought I was a narc. I told him that he could say bad things about my mother and get away with it, but calling me a narc was a death sentence unless he could prove it did not happen.

He pleaded for me to give him a chance to prove it did not happen and he would make it up to me. I told him I had to go back to Texas for a few days and when

I return, if I even heard someone breathe the word narc, I would be at his house!

The following week I bought about fifty percent of all the drugs I bought during the entire operation!

Another episode comes to mind that happened in this span of time and that was when I was riding around with three guys that I had made cases on. Charles asked me if I wanted a hit off of his weed. I told him if I did that I would choke to death because I did not even smoke cigarettes!

I told him to give me a hit of acid as I could handle that! He gave me a small pill that was later identified as a purple microdot. I pretended to take it with a big slug of beer. We were just driving around town and it was raining like hell, about nine thirty or so in the evening, when we came to a traffic signal. I thought this would be a good time to make "believers" of the guys in the car. I opened the door halfway through the intersection and fell onto the street, lying on my back yelling: "WOW look at the lights and all the colors!!" The guys in the car jumped out yelling at me: "You're going to get the cops on us! Get back in the car!!" They then took me back to my car and left me there. This little ruse made believers out of them and they began selling me different kind of pills and other drugs.

I still remember at the end of the operation (which was called Operation Sunbelt,) when every deputy and local police officer in the area took part in rounding up those who were indicted.

They were taken to the county jail and booked. I was inside a room where I could see them but they could not see me. I had to identify them as the officers brought them in.

About two weeks later I went to the Sheriff's office to testify against one of the subjects. I had to walk through the jail area. Ralph, who was still in custody, saw me and just lost it. He called me every dirty name he could think of and "lousy narc" was one of them! What can I say?

All of the defendants plead guilty or were found guilty by jury trials in the preceding months. Many of them received heavy sentences.

MADISON COUNTY

It was in July of 1983 that I met with Mr. Robert Mitchell of the Madison County prosecutor's office. We came to an agreement to work a covert operation similar to the one I ran in Logan County.

One of the trusted friends of Mr. Mitchell owned an old abandoned fuel station just outside of London, Ohio, near the middle of the county. Geographically, it was the perfect location to set up shop.

I had a sign made (to hang outside of the building) with the name of the construction company that I was going to use during this ruse. I parked my camper right behind the station where I would be living during this job.

The first week or two, I spent a lot of time just going into taverns and bars, getting to know people and letting them know who I was and the company I worked for.

I let it be known that I was taking applications at the local motel for a couple of days. I was playing pool with them, throwing darts, and just generally screwing around, knowing that sooner or later someone would bring up smoking a joint or doing a line of cocaine.

As time went on I found that the hub for the kind of people that I wanted to be dealing with was a bar in

West Jefferson, Ohio called Whitey's. It was pretty much downtown, the beer flowed very well and the people were friendly enough.

It wasn't very long until I began getting tight with some of the locals. I began taking a few gals out to dinner and dancing with them at the bars. I would buy them drinks and play pool with them.

I very cautiously brought up the fact that I used pot on occasion and once in a great while I did some acid. I mentioned that I was having a hard time replenishing my supply because my "go to man" had gotten busted by the law in North Carolina. He was trying to raise bail money so he could meet up with me here in Ohio.

Kendall Contractors (a fictitious company that I had made up for this drug investigation.) was headquartered out of North Carolina.

At the same time I was working this drug sting, I was asked by a fellow police officer from Hillsboro, Ohio, if I would be willing to help give him some training on how to set up and proceed with a drug investigation. I swore I would never work with a partner ever again, but this guy was not only a police officer, he was my friend.

This officer's name was Joe Powell and had worked with me on the Seaman, Ohio police department. We had worked many burglary and other criminal investigations together in and around Seaman. Joe only came to the area of my covert operation on a very limited basis. Mainly because I liked working by myself and because he had to work his regular job.

The few times that he went with me, he had done a very good job. There was just a couple of mistakes and only one that could have created a problem with the covert operation.

We were playing pool at Whitey's bar and having a good time when Joe slipped and called me by my last name. I picked up on it right away and kept playing as though I never heard him, and hoped that no one else did.

It was the only time that I had to chastise him during any of the times he worked with me. I know he still remembers it to this day. I had met with him while working on this book and we talked about this particular covert operation.

I made cases on thirteen different subjects without any serious occurrences. I did however have my truck broken into. The culprit stole my firearm that I had hid under the seat. That firearm was just a few inches from my ID card and badge! Talk about luck!

I did take extra precautions for the next few weeks, watching for any changes in people's attitude toward me. I knew that if they figured out I was a cop, it would get around fast and would place myself and Joe in danger.

The weather was starting to get much cooler so I had to either start finding a way to stay a little warmer during the nights or bring this operation to a close. My camper did not have a good heater in it and running any kind of fuel combustion heater was out of the question!

This covert operation went well and after about five months, I testified before the Madison County, Ohio grand jury. Thirteen subjects were secretly indicted on various drug related charges.

After the indictments were handed down, the prosecutor's office obtained warrants for the thirteen subjects.

It was decided that I was going to get as many of the suspects as I could to attend a party at our favorite bar, Whitey's. I spent the first part of the week contacting and inviting all these people to the party. The reason for the party would be that I was headed to a different project site in North Carolina. I let everyone know that I would be furnishing the beer for the party.

In preparation of the free beer, I gave the manager of the bar three hundred dollars and told him that only the people wearing name tags with proper ID would be given free beer. I also advised him that if the money ran out I would give him more.

It was finally PARTY TIME! The Sheriff had put a transmitter on my back so his officers would know when I gave the "go ahead" to raid the place. The Sheriff had his officer's in place, as near the bar as they could be and still remain unseen. When the Sheriff heard me say "all is here that is going to be here", he and all his officers would go ahead with the raid.

About nine forty five p.m. most everyone we had warrants for, was there at the party. I gave the pre-arranged signal for the raid to begin.

About that time, my friend Joe decided he had to go to the restroom. He slid from the stool he was sitting on and headed toward the back of the bar. I tried to call him back because I knew what was coming! Joe was about to meet a very big dog and an even bigger deputy! When they came through that back door, Joe got the surprise of his life! He turned and headed back to his seat.

For some unknown reason, Joe put his hands in his pockets and the deputy, not knowing who he was, began yelling at him to get his hands out of his pockets and get against the wall!

Now Joe, being a police officer, knew the routine. He assumed the position like he had been down that road before!

It only took a few seconds and the bar was full of police and police dogs. Everyone was made to either: get up against the walls or to lean over the tables as they began looking for the subjects that were named in the warrants.

When the deputies were coming in the doors, I saw drugs begin hitting the floor as people were trying to unload their pockets! I'm sure they did not want to get caught with them!

When the deputies got to me, I started bad mouthing them (as prearranged) so that the suspects in the bar would think that I was legit in my portrayal of a drug dealer being caught up in a drug sting. This is when Joe made the greatest exit of all and nearly had to be carried to the patrol car by two deputies! I almost went into hysteria when they had to force him in the back seat. Then they took us out of town to where we had a car parked and turned us loose.

Joe and I had to go back to town the next day to get my truck. It was still sitting behind the bar and I found it had not been touched by anyone.

After this covert operation was finished, Officer Joe Powell and his wife Bessie, my wife Barb and I took some time off and went to Florida for a well deserved vacation.

Barb and I went to Homestead, Florida to visit with some friends of ours from Manchester, Ohio. On the way, we dropped Joe and Bessie off near Orlando to visit with Bessie's sister and brother-in-law.

We spent two full weeks in Florida lying on the beaches in Key West and getting sun burned. We ate some of the finest sea food in the country at Italian Joes in the Florida Keys. We visited with our friends and did a lot of sightseeing with them.

After two short weeks, we said our farewell's to our friends and headed back to Orlando to pick up Joe and Bessie.

On arrival back to Seaman, Ohio, I continued working as a part time police officer. Since the covert operation had ended, I was in need of a full time job. I applied for a job on the Winchester, Ohio police department. They had lost an officer due to retirement. I interviewed for the job with Chief Sidders and Mayor Mr. Chuck Tumbleson. After a short council meeting, I was hired to a six month probationary period which is required by the Ohio Peace Officers Association.

FINDING MY SON

I was living in Seaman, Ohio and working as a police officer for Winchester, Ohio when my son turned sixteen years old. I figured he had most likely gotten his driver's license. I ran my sons social security number through the most likely states that I assumed Pat would have gone to. I finally located my son in the state of Florida.

I wrote him a letter telling him who I was. I sent him some photos and other proof that I was his father. I gave him my phone number and ask him to call me collect anytime.

A few days went by or maybe longer I just can't remember exactly. It was absolutely mind numbing when he called! I was scared and excited at the same time! I had a terrible time saying the right words except that I had never forgotten him and that I loved him.

I ask him if he would like to come to Ohio and visit with me and the family for awhile. He said he would like to and kept calling me sir. I ask him where he was calling from and he told me he was calling from a pay phone because his mother would not let him use the home phone to call me.

He gave me the number of the phone where he was calling from and I ask him to stay there until I called him back. When I called him back, I advised him that I had purchased him air fare to Cincinnati, Ohio and we would pick him up on his arrival.

When his flight arrived, we were all watching for him. Since we had not seen him for sixteen years we wondered if we would be able to recognize him. Lo and behold when he came out the chute, there was no doubt in anyone's mind that he was my son. I thought he looked just like me, only taller and thinner.

After picking him up I did not think we would ever stop talking. I remember trying my best not to bad mouth his mother because I knew in my heart that the divorce was mostly my fault and she **was still** his mom.

We spent the next few days just getting to know each other. We tried to fill in the details of our past. He told me how his mother had told him that she thought I was dead or had just run off someplace and could not be found. He told me how she had attempted to change his name. His name is Gary David but his driver's license says his name is David Gary. The courts would not allow her to change his name because she could not produce a death certificate proving that I was deceased.

Most teachers in school call you by your first name. I believe Pat did not want him to be called Gary and that is why she told him his name was David Gary. I produced our divorce papers and let him read for himself that his mother was the one who ran off and could not be found.

I introduced David to the sheriff of the county where I was working. While we were there, I ran an arrest record check on his step- dad and he and I both found out at the same time that he had been convicted of a serious crime. I still don't know to this day if David's mother knew this or not when she married him. I do remember her calling me all sorts of names on the phone when David asked her about it.

David stayed with us for about six or seven months then decided he wanted to go back to Florida. He had a girlfriend there and of course his mother.

It seems it was not to long after David returned to Florida that his step-dad had a coronary and passed on to a better place.

While still working at Winchester, I found it was like all other small towns when it came to who you were allowed to arrest and who you could not. Be as it may, things went well and I got along very well with most of the people in town.

While attending a meeting of the Adams County Peace Officers Association, I was advised from the sheriff's department that they had received information from Clark County that three fugitives who were wanted for a felony robbery was residing in Winchester and we should check it out.

I found out in just a couple of days where these people were staying. I got with the Chief and called Officer Joe Powell from the Seaman Police department to assist. Upon Joe's arrival, we executed the search warrants and arrested them without any incidents. They were taken to the sheriff's office to be detained until the Clark County officers could come and get them.

At the end of my six month probationary period, the council requested that I continue working under the probationary status for a while longer. They were still evaluating my job and trying to determine if the town could continue to be able to financially afford my position.

After listening to them talk, I began reading the writing on the wall and accepted the lay off in a graceful manner.

I took a job with the Pinkerton Security services and went to the Martin County Coal mines in the state of Kentucky, as a strike force team member.

Now this job only lasted for about four weeks or until the minors settled their strike with the owners of the mines. It was dark and really, really quite on that guard post at night. The only excitement that I encountered was when I was backing out of the motel; I backed into the side of a pickup truck!

When that job was over, I traveled back to Seaman and began drawing unemployment for a while.

While drawing my unemployment I continued to look for work as a peace officer. I also was an instructor in the martial arts. One of my students in the martial arts class told me that Lake Waynoka, (a property owners association) was looking for Rangers to patrol the gated community. Rangers had all the authority of a regular peace officer. Lake Waynoka was located in Brown County, Ohio

So I went to Lake Waynoka and spoke with the Chief Ranger, John Morgan and made application for the position. The application was then taken to the Associations board of directors and I was hired a short time later.

THE WAY WE
WERE

LAKE WAYNOKA

Being the lowest man on the totem pole, I had to work through the Christmas holiday of 1984-1985. It was very quiet around the lakes because everyone was with family & friends. Just to pass the time away, I had been looking through the time cards of all the officers. I noticed that the Chief was putting down days that he claimed he worked when in reality he was somewhere else on the planet! This was called falsifying time cards, which is against all rules and ethics of a police officer!

I made copies of the cards and continued watching the time cards for another month or so. I found three or four more violations and made copies of those. I gave them to the manager of the association advising him of the discrepancies.

In just a couple of weeks the Chief was terminated from his position. Rightfully so! It's sad to say, but I still believe to this day that I was let go because I turned the Chief in.

My wife Barb was also working for Lake Waynoka during this time and I did not want to cause a problem with her job, so I just went on my merry way.

I signed up for unemployment and began doing short term drug investigations for Key II Security of Troy, Ohio.

Now is when I decided to freeze my police pension and give up working as a commissioned police officer.

To me it was a wonderful experience to attain all that I did up to this time of my life. I felt I had accomplished my goal. I had proved to myself and to the world that a guy could get into serious trouble: but with a whole lot of patience and hard work he can overcome the bad times and make something of himself.

Not only did I become a full time street police officer in 1975, I was inducted into the Police Hall of Fame and was awarded the John Edgar Hoover Memorial Police Service Award from the State of Ohio on May 15, 1981.

What an honor for a guy who was once convicted of a felony and twenty three years later became a commissioned police office for the same state!

I was commissioned as a Notary Public in 1979 by the then Governor James A. Rhoads and have maintained that status to this day. I also attained my ultimate goal of becoming a **Chief of Police**! I currently am a state registered employee of Key II Security in Troy, Ohio.

After freezing my retirement, I was ask to help in a couple of drug investigations in Miami and Shelby County, Ohio. See! When you're as good of an undercover agent as I was, the jobs just kept coming even though I didn't want them to!

These operations were small jobs compared to others I had done. These investigations only lasted a short time and netted about nineteen suspected drug dealers. These suspects were small time street peddlers. Yes, even these small time dealers need to be off of the streets!

FROZEN RETIREMENT

In 1986 after giving up my law enforcement career, I decided to move to the state of Florida and just get away from it all for awhile. I packed up the old motor home and our two youngest daughters and headed south!

A friend of mine, Mr. Don Bradford, who had been the Village Clerk of Manchester, Ohio during my tenure as Chief of Police, had moved to Florida the previous year.

The wife, who was working as a police officer for the Lake Waynoka Property Owners Association, stayed behind with our oldest daughter. Barb was going to sell our home, take care of other personal business then join us in Florida, later.

On arrival in Homestead Florida, I parked the motor home behind my friend's house. We ran a water hose from his house to our motor home for water and plugged in the extension cord for electricity. We were set to go!

I spent the following week getting the two girls enrolled in the school system. I found the school personnel to be very courteous but hard to understand. It was hard to find anyone who could speak good English, including the local police!

I found a job very soon after arriving in Homestead. I took a job working as a maintenance supervisor. The company made cabinets for institutions like schools and prisons. There were thirty five employees and only eight of them spoke fluent English.

I quickly picked up on how to count to ten in Spanish. I learned a few other choice words that would get most of their attention if need be.

I found it quite interesting that there were Cubans, Haitians, and other Spanish speaking workers all together in one place, because for the most part, they hated each other! It seemed that every day I was breaking up a fight or two. Some of the fights involved knives but mostly just fisticuffs.

One story sticks in my mind that happened while I worked there and it involved a young man whose name was Terry.

Now, Terry was the "go to" guy. Terry's job was to keep the routers working properly. Routers are a tool that's used to finish the corners of the tables and counter tops that was manufactured there.

If a router quit working, Terry would take it to the shop and totally dismantle it. He would rebuild it with new bearings, armature brushes and anything else that needed repaired. He would always lay out each part in precise order as he took the router apart. This made it easier for him to put it back together.

Now he was working on one of these things when he got called out to do something else in the shop. I, being the jokester that I am, had this little shiny brass washer in my pocket. I put it in amongst the parts that he had so precisely laid out.

When he returned to finish the router, I inconspicuously watched as he proceeded to reassemble the tool. I almost lost it and began to laugh as he spent fifteen or twenty minutes trying to figure out where that little shiny brass washer went.

He tried fitting it on every little shaft, screw or bolt that he had on the table! I couldn't take it anymore! I finally walked over and ask if he had seen a small brass washer that I had lost. He replied with a sarcastic look on his face, "You are a sorry ass for doing that to me!"

When my wife joined us in Florida, we moved into an apartment. She worked for an answering service for a while. We both hated the hot weather. The humidity was horrible! It seemed to rain every day even though it didn't last long. I believe we lived there for about six months and we could not take the heat anymore. To me, South Florida was a great place to visit but not to live in. We packed up the motor home again and headed back to Ohio.

14/02/2014

MIAMI VALLEY PAPER

In July 1986 I returned with my family to Ohio. I called Key II Security and went back to work for them. I started a covert operation in August of that year. I was placed in a paper mill called Millen Industries located in Franklin, Ohio.

I was actually hired by the Company's Vice President and placed into the maintenance department so I could freely move about the company. My job was to look for employees who were stealing from the company and or doing illegal acts on company property.

By the end of September, I had made a detailed report to Mr. Harper as to who in the company was violating the company policies and procedures.

Most of the activities that were being done were being done by supervisors. Since they were supervisors, they were in a position to make purchases for the company. The purchases they were making had nothing to do with the paper mill!

I could not figure out how the plant manager could walk into the maintenance shop and see boat motors being worked on! They had to know that boat motors had nothing to do with the production of coated paper!

I guess he just did not care or was too stupid to know.

The parts for the repairs on the boat motors were bought and charged to: fake repairs on lift trucks and tow motors.

One supervisor drank on the job from the time he got to work until the time he left for the day! This guy later died from injuries he suffered after he stuck his head over a large vat of flammable colored paper coating, with a lit cigarette in his mouth! I don't mean to speak ill of the dead, but if he hadn't been inebriated, he may be alive today!

One employee was hauling aluminum winding drums out the back door during the night and selling them at the local metal recycle center. Another employee was trading and selling firearms on company time and company property.

A short time after I gave the report to Mr. Harper, a few employees were terminated and some received reprimands for their stupid deeds. Some employees actually held onto their jobs because of their expertise in their job. It would have taken too long to find and retrain a replacement. The company felt it was not worth the time and cost.

On October the 4th 1986, my life changed forever. It was my daughter Christy's 16th birthday and we had planned a surprise birthday party for her.

Her boyfriend wanted to take her to town so she could pick out a gift for herself. We told them it was ok to go and they headed for the K-Mart store in

Middletown, Ohio.

The wife and I decided that while they were gone, we would run to town; pick up the cake and decorations for the party, so we could have it all set up when she got home.

While we were in the store shopping for the decorations, we heard sirens and a lot of commotion going on down the street. We did not think anything out of the ordinary and continued shopping then headed home.

Upon our arrival, our oldest daughter Misty came running to us before we could get out of the car. She said the hospital had called and said that Christy had been involved in an auto accident and we needed to get to the hospital as quick as we could.

We took off for the Middletown Regional Hospital as fast as legally possible and on arrival found that our lives was going to make a drastic change that no one could imagine. The accident caused life changing injuries to our daughter.

I was working the covert operation at the paper mill when this accident happened to our daughter. The Vice President of the paper mill was so kind to keep me on (even after the covert operation was finished) so that my daughter would continue to be insured. After eight years of care at a cost of one million dollars (the maximum coverage), we were forced to place her in a nursing facility.

This accident totally ended my law enforcement career. I had a whole new role to take on. That role was seeing that our daughter was given the best of care. I went through a lot of government red tape and dealt with insurance problems. This left very little time for other things and the rest of my family.

All the accomplishments that I have achieved and the fact I was able to write this book, "From Dark to Narc" was a direct result of my daughter's accident. Her accident also opened up many more accomplishments in my life. But that is another book.

AFTERWORD

LETTERS TO GARY

A Letter To Gary From His Youngest Daughter

All my life I have been "the baby" of the family.
The last born and probably the most spoiled.

I would like to take a moment and tell you a little about my daddy through the eyes of a child.

My dad was and is the ULTIMATE DADDY. I know every child thinks their daddy is the best, but I can honestly say my dad rates at the top. From teaching me about cars to teaching me about love and life. I am the woman I am today because of his guidance.

This book will tell you a lot about his life, and how he became the man he is today, but what it will not tell you is how he selflessly shaped the lives of his children. It came natural to our dad. He was born to teach and be a leader. His lessons weren't always easy but he always made his point. I wish I could tell you that I was the best little girl ever and never got into trouble, but my daddy taught me to never lie..... With that being said, he taught me how to be a great mom. I never realized the lessons I was learning as a child was to shape me into the woman I am today.

MY GREAT PROTECTOR

When I was just five years old, my dad became my Sensei. He taught me how to protect myself, all the while teaching me how to protect my family. It wasn't easy being the "Chief's" daughter. So, he made sure we could protect ourselves in case of any danger. He was harder on me than the other students. I never understood why until the day someone tried to grab me. **Then I knew!**

So I would like to thank my dad, for everything he has done, good or bad. Because the man he was has brought him to the man he is: My Dad.

"The Baby"
Aka Heather

A letter to Gary From His Wife Barbara

When I first met you, I thought you were the most handsome man I had ever laid eyes on. You were exactly what I always dreamed a man should be (on the outside), tall, dark and handsome.

You were such a go-getter and leader. That scared me somewhat because I was so naive compared to you. On the other hand, it was a quality in you that I liked. They say: opposites sometimes attract.

At age twenty five I figured you would be more grown up and settled in your life than what you were. I was always trying to make you more grown up and be more responsible than what you wanted to be. You always said, "You're as old as you feel and you felt like you were a teenager!"

My brother said you were "crazy" and I should turn and run the other way and not marry you! My parents did not like you at first either! They just didn't know you like I knew you. They knew you from the outside, I knew you from my heart. After forty five years of marriage, I think that proves them all to be wrong in their assessment of you!

When we first married, I was unsure if I had done the

right thing even though my heart told me I had. When our first born arrived, you were such a proud daddy! The same was true when the next two were born. Four females and one male in a home was tough. You always gave in to the girls. They had you wrapped around their fingers for the most part. You also gave me another daughter and a son from your previous marriages, which I love very much. I never considered them my step-children nor did I call myself their step-mother. We were just one big happy family when they were around and I will always cherish those times with them.

Our children gave us grand-children and as of this writing, one awesome great-grandson. It all started with our love for each other. Two of our girls have grown up to be outstanding wives, mothers, grandmother and upstanding women in their communities. Our middle daughter (who is disabled from an accident) is the apple of your eye and I'm so proud of how you have been my rock through her ordeal.

I was so proud of you when you accepted Christ as your personal Saviour. I also believe that was when my parents really started liking you. God can work wonders with a man's soul if he will just let Him. We have had many tests and trials in our forty five years of marriage. There were times that I just "wanted to leave" the marriage because of "not knowing" why you were doing the things that you were doing. But somewhere deep in my heart I know that God brought us together and I knew He would see me through those tests and trials.

Gary, the world may know you as a criminal who turned his life around and made something of himself, but I know you as a loving husband, a wonderful father, grandfather and great grandfather. You are a "jack-of-all-trades" and a master of all of them too. I know your father played a huge roll in that. You may have had many jobs over the years and "yes" that was hard to deal with. But, you always provided for your family. We may not have had all of our wants, but we had all of our needs provided for.

Gary, I just want everyone to know that this book does NOT portray the man that you are today! I am glad that I did not know you during your younger days because I would have run in the opposite direction! God had a plan for your life and mine. He just wanted the time to be right. Lastly, I just want you to know that I love you with all of my heart and soul.

Your Wife,
Barbara

Acknowledgments

"Thanks" to the greatest parents who have stuck by my side through all of my misgivings, stupid and illegal acts, divorces and even the good times.

"Thanks" to Michael Stahr for his continual prodding to get me to put my life's story in book form. "Thanks" for answering all the stupid computer questions I had. "Thanks" for all the computer work you have done in getting this book into first and final gear.

Special "thanks" to my wife for sticking with me after all of my screw-up's and for all the times I lived away from home. "Thanks" for all the prayers you sent to God, on my behalf.

"Thanks" to all of my children: Linda, Gary David, Misty, Christy and my baby daughter, Heather for all of their help. I know there were times when you didn't think I knew what I was doing. You just "bit your tongue" and helped me anyhow.

"Thanks" to my granddaughters Courtney and Madison for all of their computer expertise and helping me with my English. It was not one of my favorite subjects, which made this journey more difficult.

"Thanks" to Terry Brewer for her help in creating the cover for the book. "Thanks" for all of your computer expertise also.

Made in the USA
Charleston, SC
15 June 2014